People solve problems by inventing new things.

SCHOLASTIC
LITERACY
PLACE®

Copyright acknowledgments and credits appear on page 136, which constitutes an extension of this copyright page.

Copyright © 1996 by Scholastic Inc.   All rights reserved.   Printed in the U.S.A.
                                             ISBN 0-590-48907-0

          6 7 8 9 10   24   02 01 00

World's first shoe made from recycled materials

Visit an Inventor's Office

People solve problems by inventing new things.

New and Improved

Many inventions have improved people's lives.

3533 McNair Way
Lexington, KY 40513
September 7, 1994

Poppo's Pizza
238 Sitwell Place
San Francisco, CA 94179

To May Concern:

Inventors at Work

Inventors problem-solve as they work.

The Handy Helper
flexible magnet
velcro fastens it to wrist
magnetic bracelet
holds nails and t...

Fast Forward

Inventors try to make the future better.

Trade Books

The following
books accompany this
What an Idea!
SourceBook.

Fiction

**Danny Dunn
and the
Homework
Machine**

by Jay Williams
and Raymond
Abrashkin
illustrated by
Ezra Jack Keats

AWARD WINNING Book

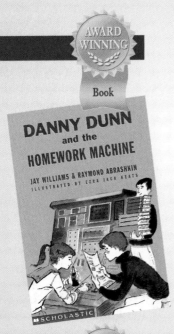

Nonfiction

**Eureka!
It's an
Airplane!**

by Jeanne
Bendick
illustrated by
Sal Murdocca

AWARD WINNING Author

Classic Fiction

**On the Banks of
Plum Creek**

by Laura Ingalls
Wilder
illustrated by
Garth Williams

AWARD WINNING Book

Biography

The Real McCoy

by Wendy Towle
illustrated by
Wil Clay

AWARD WINNING Book

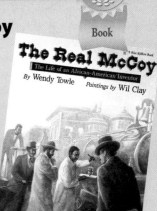

EARLY HOT-AIR BALLOON

YOW!

PENICILLIN DISCOVERED IN 1928

? !

EARLY TELEPHONE

Many inventions have improved people's lives.

New and Improved

Travel along a time line that highlights famous inventions. Next, follow a piece of string through the centuries.

Learn how the first sneaker was invented.

Find out how Julie Lewis turned garbage into shoes.

WORKSHOP 1

Tell a company how it could improve its product.

3533 McNair Way
Lexington, KY 40513
September 7, 1999

Poppe's Pizza
238 Sitwell Place
San Francisco, CA 94174

To Whom It May Concern:

Your frozen pizza really hits the spot, but there aren't enough pieces. Instead of four pieces in each pizza, why not eight? You could make your pizza a little bigger and make your pieces smaller. All the kids would

Amazing

B.C.

3500s B.C.

The wheel is invented by the Sumerians in what is now Iraq.

A.D.

A.D. 100s

Paper is invented in China by Ts'ai Lun. Knowledge of papermaking eventually spread to Europe by way of the Islamic world.

A.D. 200s

The Maya are the first to use the number zero.

Mayan 0

A.D. 1280s

Eyeglasses are developed in Italy.

A.D. 1450s

The printing press is invented in Germany.

INVENTIONS & DISCOVERIES

1593

Galileo Galilei devises the first thermometer.

1656

The first successful pendulum clock is invented by Christiaan Huygens. This clock improved the accuracy of timekeeping.

1783

The Montgolfier brothers are the first to construct and ride in a hot-air balloon in France.

1809

Mary Dixon Kies becomes the first woman to receive a U.S. patent for her invention of a weaving process.

1871

Margaret Knight invents a machine that makes paper bags. She later patents 21 more inventions.

1   *2*   *3*   *4*

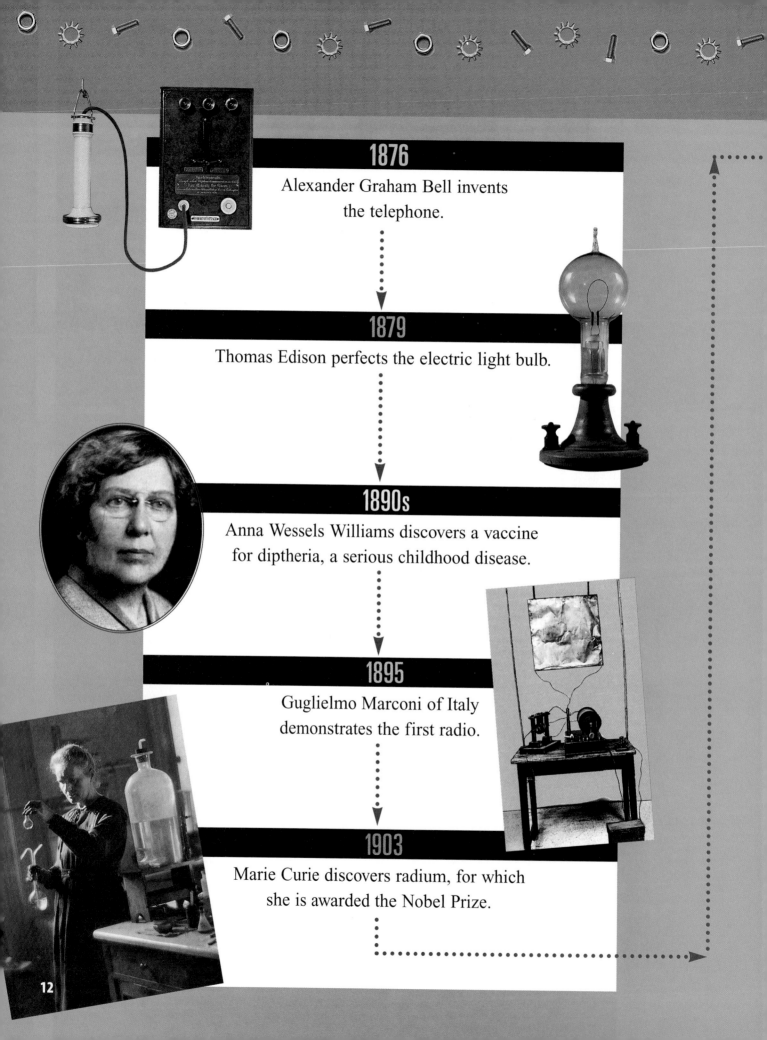

1876

Alexander Graham Bell invents the telephone.

1879

Thomas Edison perfects the electric light bulb.

1890s

Anna Wessels Williams discovers a vaccine for diptheria, a serious childhood disease.

1895

Guglielmo Marconi of Italy demonstrates the first radio.

1903

Marie Curie discovers radium, for which she is awarded the Nobel Prize.

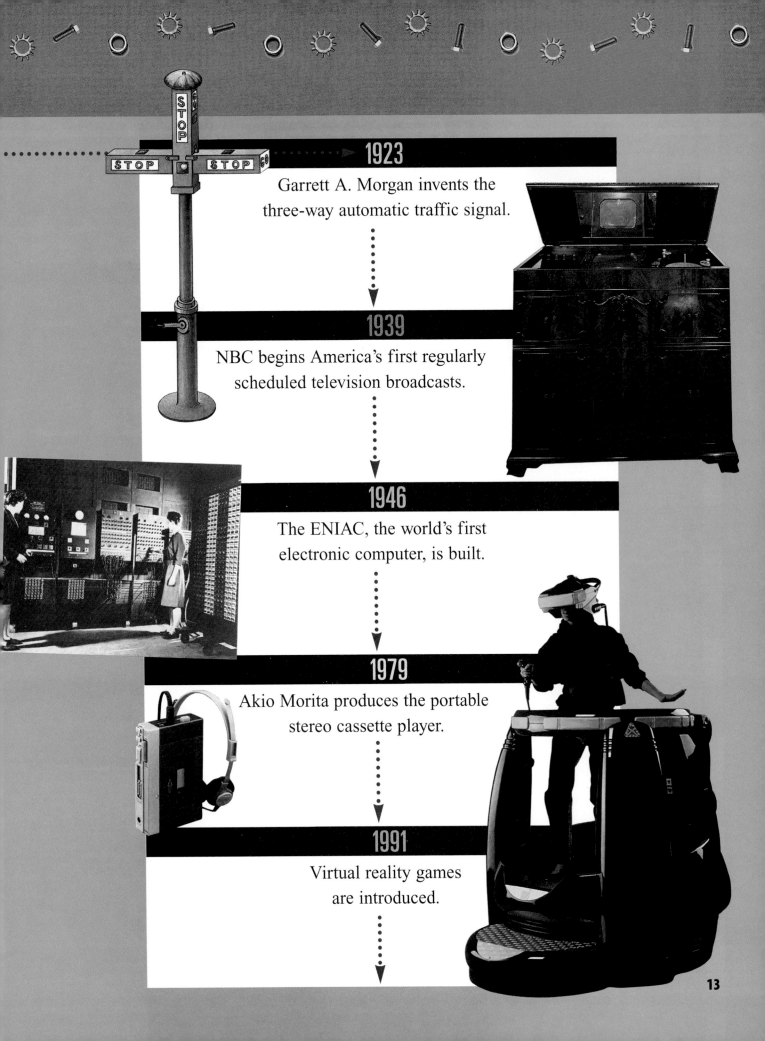

1923

Garrett A. Morgan invents the three-way automatic traffic signal.

1939

NBC begins America's first regularly scheduled television broadcasts.

1946

The ENIAC, the world's first electronic computer, is built.

1979

Akio Morita produces the portable stereo cassette player.

1991

Virtual reality games are introduced.

13

A PIECE of STRING

IS A WONDERFUL THING

by **JUDY HINDLEY**   illustrated by **MARGARET CHAMBERLAIN**

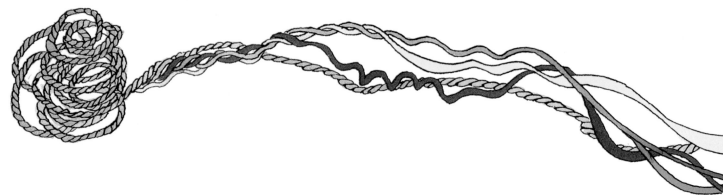

AWARD WINNING

Author

*W*hat a wonderful
thing string is!
Just think of the things
you can do with string!

14

Let us sing a song
about string—
what a wonderful thing it is!
When you think of the things
that you do with string,
you have to admit
it's a marvelous bit
to have in your kit:

My friend's uncle said, "You should never go anywhere without change for a phone call, a pencil stub, and a piece of string."

for a fishing line, a boat, a kite,
somewhere to hang your socks to dry;
for tying up packages, fastening gates,
leading you safe through a treacherous cave;
for a spinning top, a skipping rope,
a bracelet, a necklace, a drawstring purse . . .
there's just about no end of things
a person can do with a piece of string!
And then you wonder,
from time to time,
how did a thing like
string begin?

← slipknot

A slipknot can hitch
a boat, a horse,
a swing...

three small knots   three big knots   three small knots

= . . . — — — . . .
= Morse code for S.O.S.

In New Guinea, people make fishing nets out of spiderwebs. They leave a wooden frame with a colony of spiders, who spin their webs around it. In the British Museum, I saw a spiderweb hat that was made this way.

Back in the days
when mammoths roamed,
and they didn't have chains
and they didn't have ropes
for hauling around or
lifting things up—

(well, they didn't have any connecting things:
buttons or braces or buckles or laces,
or latches or catches or bolts or belts,
or tabs or clasps or hooks and eyes . . .
Velcro patches! ribbons! ties!
zips or grips or snaps or clips)—
well how did anyone
THINK IT UP?

Did they chat as they sat
near the fire at night,
eating their prehistoric fish,
and say, "What we need
to get it right
is a thing like hair,
but long and strong,
a thing to tie on a piece of bone:
what a wonderful fishing line
that would make!"?

After which, I suppose,
they went out to the lake
and tickled the fish
with their cold, bare hands—
for they didn't have nets
if they didn't have string.
How they all must have wished
that they had such a thing!

For a long time the only spears were pointed sticks.
Much later, a chip of stone would be tied to
the stick with a sinew.

So how on earth
do you think they discovered it?
Do you think somebody
just tripped over it?
Was it an accident?
Was it a guess?
Did it emerge
from a hideous mess?
Did it begin with
a sinuous twig,
a whippety willow,
a snaky vine?

Did it happen that somebody,
one dark night,
winding his weary way home alone,
got tripped by the foot on a loop of vine
and fell kersplat! and broke a bone;
and then, as he lay in the dark, so sad,
and yelled for help (and it didn't come)
he got thoroughly bored with doing that
and invented—a woolly-rhinoceros trap?

In order to hunt successfully, people had to start working as a team.
But there's always a slowpoke . . .

Oh, it might have occurred
in a number of ways
as the populace pondered
the fate they faced—
as they huddled in caves
in the worst of the weather,
wishing for things like
tents
and clothes,
as they hugged furry skins
to their shivering bodies
and scraps of hide
to their cold, bare toes

And they had no suspenders
or snaps or connectors
or buttons or toggles
or zippers or pins—
so HOW did they hold up
their trousers, then?
They must have said,
"Oh! A piece of string
would be SUCH a fine thing
to have around the cave!"

Teams of hunters drove their prey over cliffs
or possibly into holes hidden by vines.

They needed a noose for an antelope foot.
They needed a thing to string a bow.
They needed nets, and traps, and snares
for catching their venison unaware
and leading the first wild horses home.

A single fiber of wool is as strong as a thread of gold.

SPINNING A THIN THING FROM A FAT THING

Yarn is spun from sheep's fleece, cotton tufts, or even birds' down.

Try spinning with cotton. Pull and stretch it very gently, very steadily, twisting it really tight as it draws out.

Well, they must've gone on to try and try
as hundreds of thousands of years went by,
twisting and braiding and trying out knots
with strips of hide and rhinoceros guts,
spiders' webs and liana vines,
reeds and weeds and ribs of palm,
slippery sinews, muscles, and thongs,
elephant grasses three feet long,
and wriggly fish-bone skeletons.

And they spun out the fibers
of vegetable fluff,
and they felted the hairs of a goat,
and they knitted and twisted
and braided and twined

and invented . . .

TURNING A THIN THING INTO A FLAT THING
The next trick is weaving and knitting to make fabric.
Tiny short hairs laid down higgledy-piggledy, then
wetted and pressed together, can be turned into felt.

23

the three-ply rope!
What a wonderful thing!
A very fine thing!
The KING of string
is rope!

You can lift up pots
from an echoing well with it,
fling it to make a bridge;
you can haul along hulking hunks
of stone for building a pyramid
(and they did).

The Egyptians made rope from bulrushes, camel hair, and flax.

The oldest rope ever discovered came from a tomb in Egypt. It was made from flax 5000 years ago.

Sometimes rope was even made from women's hair.

You can also halter and harness
your animal friends.

And then again, when life gets tough
and it's time to be moving along,
you can use it to lash your luggage fast
to a camel, a goat, a raft, a boat—
oh! a stringable thing
is the only thing
to have when you're afloat!

Making Rope

One man twists
two strands
clockwise and
walks forward.

A second man
makes
sure the strands
of rope are laid
tightly together.

A third man
closes the
strands by
twisting this tool
counterclockwise
and walks backward
as the rope is
formed.

But they still
went on and on,
sticking and spinning
and looping and gluing
and tying and trying out
more and more types,
quicker and quicker
crazier, slicker

early cart

The pontoon bridge was an
early bright idea. It began
with a row of boats
all roped together.

Roman crane

early gravity railway

Isambard Kingdom Brunel went up in a hot-air balloon to lay the first rope of the famous Clifton Suspension Bridge in Bristol, England.

early flying machine

Hot metal can be stretched into rails and cables, ropes, and delicate wires.

for pulleys and ladders
and hoses and bridges
and fences and winches
and wires and pipes.

27

Where on earth
have we come to now?
What would a town
ever do without string
and things that go stringing along?
Candlewicks, rackets, and violins,
telephones, plumbing, and railroad lines,
things that fasten and fuse and fix
and click and stick and link.

Can you even begin
to count the ways
that things connect
with other things?
It could just about
scramble your brain!

And to think it began
(though we'll never know when)
with somebody choking
on elephant gristle,
or trying to chew
through the stem
of a thistle,
or just stumbling into
the thing!

Oh, what we've done
with a piece of string
is a marvelous thing,
an amazing thing—
some would say
a crazy thing!
And one of these days
I might just go away
and begin it
all over
again . . .

from Steven Caney's

Invention Book

The Invention of

Sneakers

How rubber-soled shoes with canvas uppers became known as "sneaks" or "sneakers" is not exactly known. The reason may be the obvious one—rubber and canvas shoes are very quiet. But the phenomenal popularity of the sneaker has more to do with its comfort and style than with the ability to sneak around quietly.

The story of the rubber-soled sneaker begins with the development of rubber. For many centuries, the natives of Central and South America commonly used the gum that oozed from the bark of certain trees to cover and protect the bottoms of their feet. Their technique was to apply the gum directly in thin layers, curing each layer with gentle heat from a fire. The result was a coating that covered the bottom of the wearer's foot and protected it from rough land.

SNEAKERS

A British traveler, in the late 1700s, became fascinated with these strange-looking foot coverings, but he was even more intrigued with the possibility of using the gum to make other products. He collected several samples of the gum and the products the natives made from it and returned to England, where he showed the new substance to his chemist friend Joseph Priestley. Priestley's first discovery was that the gum had the unique ability to cleanly erase pencil marks by briskly rubbing the paper with it—so he enthusiastically named the substance "rubber."

For the next fifty years, several products made of rubber were manufactured—mostly water-proof containers and coverings to protect all kinds of things from the rain. And by 1820 someone finally designed a rubber cover that the wearer could stretch over his leather shoes to protect them in wet or muddy weather. These rubber "overshoes" quickly found their way to America, and the new novelty product became an instant success—but not for long.

This drawing shows how the Mayans made shoes by covering their feet with melted rubber.

SNEAKERS

In an attempt to make money on the popular imported fad, many New England shoe manufacturers hastily set up factories, making rubber overshoes in various styles that incorporated hand-painted designs and other decorations. But within just a few years the attraction had diminished, as wearers soon discovered that pure rubber became obnoxiously smelly and sticky in hot weather, and brittle enough to crack into small pieces during cold weather. By 1823 no one wanted anything to do with rubber overshoes.

About that time, Charles Goodyear, a young out-of-work hardware salesman, decided to take on the challenge of eliminating rubber's shortcomings. Goodyear's interest became a hobby and then a serious undertaking. Soon he was dedicating all his time and money to making rubber a more stable product. Goodyear believed that the solution involved adding certain chemicals to the pure rubber gum and finding the right way to cure the mixture.

Experiment after experiment failed, and Charles Goodyear went broke. He borrowed money from friends and businessmen, but he still couldn't find the right formula. Eventually Goodyear was arrested and put into debtor's prison for failing to pay back his creditors.

While the shoe industry still tried to bring back the fad by introducing various new styles of rubber overshoes, the sticky, smelly, and often brittle substance found little acceptance as footwear. In 1834 an inventor named Wait Webster patented a process for attaching rubber to the soles of shoes and boots with uppers made of leather, but the combination did nothing to eliminate the original problems with rubber.

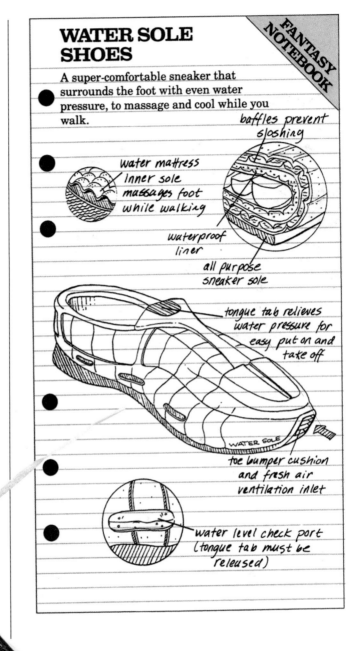

FANTASY NOTEBOOK

WATER SOLE SHOES

A super-comfortable sneaker that surrounds the foot with even water pressure, to massage and cool while you walk.

baffles prevent sloshing

water mattress inner sole massages foot while walking

waterproof liner

all purpose sneaker sole

tongue tab relieves water pressure for easy put on and take off

WATER SOLE

toe bumper cushion and fresh air ventilation inlet

water level check port (tongue tab must be released)

An artist's rendition of Charles Goodyear at work, just as he discovered the process of vulcanization.

By 1838 Charles Goodyear was at his experiments again; this time another rubber enthusiast, Nathaniel Hayward, joined him. They discovered that if they mixed sulfur with the gum rubber and then left it in the sun to bake slowly, the mixture would form a rubbery but not sticky outer skin. Goodyear was sure he was on the track to the solution, but Hayward wasn't so convinced. So Goodyear paid Hayward for his contribution and optimistically went on experimenting alone.

One year later, Charles Goodyear got lucky. He was mixing up a batch of gum rubber, sulfur, and white lead when a glob of the mixture fell off his stirring utensil and onto the hot stovetop. When the mass cooled and Goodyear went to remove it, he discovered that the rubber had cured perfectly—consistently rubbery through-out and not sticky at all! He then discovered that his new "metallic" rubber (he called it "metallic" because of the lead in the mixture) was more elastic and considerably less brittle. Goodyear named the process for making metallic rubber vulcanization, after the Roman god of fire, Vulcan.

Now that a better rubber had been invented, a better rubber shoe could be made. Charles Goodyear licensed his vulcanization process to several shoe companies and also to manufacturers of all types of rubber products. Some companies made rubber-soled shoes, rubber shoe covers, or even all-rubber shoes, and one shoe manufacturer, Thomas Crane Wales, made a waterproof boot of rubberized cloth with a rubber sole, called "Wales patent Arctic gaitors." But the first real sneaker with laced canvas uppers and vulcanized rubber soles came in 1868 from the Candee Manufacturing Company of New Haven, Connecticut. These canvas-and-rubber "croquet sandals" were made to appeal strictly to the wealthy, and they were sold through the exclusive Peck and Snyder Sporting Goods Catalog.

Fortunately, the Candee Company's marketing scheme didn't work as planned, and people who never thought of playing croquet began wearing the light and comfortable canvas-and-rubber shoes. By 1873 the shoes were commonly called sneaks or sneakers. And by the beginning of the twentieth century, everyday people often wore 60¢ canvas-and-rubber sneakers, while the rich wore more expensive models with silk, satin, and white duck uppers, trimmed in bows for women and elk skin for men.

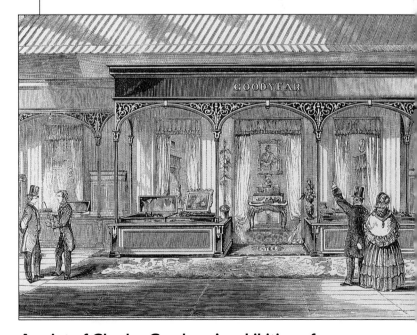

A print of Charles Goodyear's exhibition of rubber products at the famous Crystal Palace in Sydenham, England, from 1893.

SNEAKERS

While the sneaker became increasingly popular as a comfortable, stylish casual shoe, it also was being used as a sporting shoe. Special types of sneakers were being made for all kinds of popular sports and games. In 1909 the basketball sneaker was introduced, and a year later the Spalding Company invented a rubber sneaker sole with molded suction cups for better traction. In 1915 the U.S. Navy ordered non-slip sneakers to be used aboard ships.

A picture of the early Spalding tennis shoes in action.

In 1917 Henry McKinney, the public relations director for the National India Rubber Company (owned by the U.S. Rubber Company), decided it was time to call the canvas-and-rubber shoe

An early advertisement for Spalding tennis shoes.

SNEAKERS

something different from the ever-popular sneaker. After reviewing more than 300 suggestions, he selected the name "Peds" (from the Latin word meaning "foot"). However, McKinney soon discovered that another company used "Peds," and he quickly switched to the now-famous brand name "Keds." The idea worked, and for a while the Keds name was just as familiar as sneakers.

Many other companies tried to create new sneaker fads, and some succeeded. Over the past seventy-odd years, "new, improved" models have appeared with features such as arch cushions, colored uppers, colored rubber soles, side venting outlets, waffle soles, and most recently, curved-sole "running" shoes. Today the sneaker is by far America's most popular and comfortable shoe style, accounting for over one-quarter of all shoes sold—and very few are worn for croquet.

Fantasy Inventions

The sneaker has come a long way since the early twentieth century and there is no reason you can't invent another variation on this old favorite.

Slug Glue Dispenser. A healthy live slug is placed inside the glue dispenser carrying case. When glue is needed, a portion of the case bottom is removed and the slug is allowed to walk across the area to be glued.

Shoe Shine Vending Machine. Provides a quick shoe shine for people on the move. Shine selection options include rainy day waterproofing, military spit shine, different color shade, and a computerized shoe condition report.

New Sneaker Smell Renewer. A spray that gets rid of old sneaker smell and replaces it with the smell of a new pair of shoes.

Headlight Shoes. Shoe toe headlights and red heel taillights provide safety for nighttime joggers and walkers.

Julie Lewis

Inventor

Inventor + Problem = Solution!

Julie Lewis is an inventor who cares about the environment. Her most successful invention tackles a problem that is becoming bigger every day—too much garbage. Can garbage be turned into something useful? After some experimenting, Lewis came up with a solution: shoes!

PROFILE

Name: Julie Lewis

Occupation: inventor and founder of Deja Shoe Inc.

Special skills: ability to see a problem and solve it

Favorite invention: the telephone

A problem that needs an inventive solution: air pollution

Previous jobs: bread factory worker, nutrition teacher, waitress

Favorite book in fourth grade:
Harriet the Spy by Louise Fitzhugh

QUESTIONS
for Julie Lewis

Learn how *Julie Lewis* found a practical solution to an environmental problem.

 What gave you the idea to invent shoes out of trash?

 My college roommate was in nursing school. One cold day, she hung her polyester nursing-school pants on the radiator. They melted. That's when I realized that some fabrics were made of plastics. Later, when I thought of using recycled materials to make cloth, I remembered her pants melting.

 How did that help you come up with your invention?

 It made me think of what gets recycled: aluminum, plastics, and even tire rubber. I had some sandals made from old tires, which gave me the idea of combining different types of recycled "garbage" to make shoes.

 How did you turn garbage into shoes?

 It took me a few years to develop a cloth made from recycled plastics. Then I made some model shoes with it. My two kids thought it was funny. They'd say, "Oh, there's Mom trying to invent again."

What was the next step?

 I didn't know anything about making shoes, but I wasn't afraid to ask. First I talked to Bill Bowerman, a shoe designer and co-founder of Nike Shoes. I explained my idea, and showed him what I'd done. He made me a model of the first Deja shoe.

 Did you start a company with just one shoe?

That model shoe was all I needed. I applied for a grant from an Oregon agency in charge of recycling. I presented a business plan and an explanation of how to turn recycled materials into shoes. They awarded me $110,000 to start my company.

 Do you feel that you've solved the problem of waste in the environment?

 Not at all. I'm proud of our success in recycling, but there's so much more to do!

Julie Lewis's
Tips for Young Inventors

1 Don't be discouraged if someone says your idea is dumb.

2 Look for alternative solutions. If a solution doesn't work, try another, and another, until one works.

3 Get information from experts.

How to
Write a Product Improvement Letter

The company's address ●

Did you ever buy something and think—this could be better? Did you think of different ways to improve it? Well, you can put those ideas to work in a product improvement letter.

What is a product improvement letter? A product improvement letter gives a company suggestions about how to make a more successful product. Some letters include a sketch to help illustrate the changes being suggested. Product improvement letters are usually sent to the Consumer Relations department of the company.

The letter ● ends with a closing and the writer's name.

● The return address lets the company know where to send a response.

3533 McNair Way
Lexington, KY 40513
September 7, 1994

Poppo's Pizza
238 Sitwell Place
San Francisco, CA 94179

To Whom It May Concern:

Your frozen pizza really hits the spot, but there aren't enough pieces. Instead of four pieces in each pizza, why not eight? You could make your pizza a little bigger and make each slice smaller. All the kids would think you are a super nice company.

I hope you will consider my suggestion.

Truly yours,

Daniel Otfinoski

● The body of the letter describes the product and gives suggestions.

1 Pick a Problem Product

Think of a product that needs improvement. It could be something you aren't happy with, such as a toy that doesn't work the way an advertisement promised. It could be an item you're happy with that could be made even better by adding or changing something.

TOOLS

- pen and paper
- ruler
- two envelopes
- two stamps

2 Identify Problems and Solutions

Now write two headings on a piece of paper: *Problems* and *Solutions*. Under the first heading, list all the problems with your product. It's all right if there's only one problem. Under the second heading, list ideas for solutions to make the product work better. Use a lot of details to describe the problems and solutions.

File Edit Image Camera Windows   8:55 PM
Problems/Solutions - 100%

Problems	Solutions
Too much salt	Use less salt
Not enough pretzels in bag	Put more pretzels in bag

3 Write Your Letter

Write your address and the date on the top left side of your paper.

- Skip four lines and write the address of the company on the same side.

- Skip two lines and write *Dear* _____ , (person's name). If you don't know a name, you can write *To Whom It May Concern.*

- Write a few paragraphs about how you think the product can be improved.

- Close with *Sincerely,* or *Yours truly,* followed by your signature. Print your name below your signature.

Tips
- For product improvement ideas, think of items that you use every day, such as toothpaste and shoes.
- Enclose a diagram to show how your idea would change the product.
- Be polite! A company might not respond to a rude letter.

4 Mail Your Letter

Sam Doe
23 Cherry Drive
Anywhere, Az. 09009

Consumer Re
Snack-O In
344 Food A
Gold, TN•

When you're satisfied with your letter, make a neat copy and place it in an envelope. Enclose a stamped, self-addressed envelope, so the company can send you a reply. Address, stamp, and mail your letter. You and your classmates can make a chart to track the replies you receive.

If You Are Using a Computer ...

Write your letter on the computer using the letter format. To create your own stationery, choose from the selection of letterheads.

THINK

One way to improve a product is to make it reusable. What products could be improved by making them recyclable?

Julie Lewis
Inventor ▶

I DID IT!

CHINE

Inventors at Work

Laugh out loud as Homer solves the problem of an out-of-control doughnut machine.

See how inventors turn mistakes into successes. Then read a poem about an inventor's "new" kind of flying machine.

WORKSHOP 2

Draw a diagram of an invention of your own.

Nathan Matter:
The Handy Helper

flexible magnet

velcro fastens it to wrist
magnetic bracelet

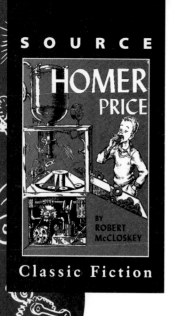

AWARD
WINNING

Book

from

Homer Price By Robert McCloskey

THE DOUGHNUTS

ne Friday night in November Homer overheard his mother talking on the telephone to Aunt Agnes over in Centerburg. "I'll stop by with the car in about half an hour and we can go to the meeting together," she said, because tonight was the night the Ladies' Club was meeting to discuss plans for a box social and to knit and sew for the Red Cross.

"I think I'll come along and keep Uncle Ulysses company while you and Aunt Agnes are at the meeting," said Homer.

So after Homer had combed his hair and his mother had looked to see if she had her knitting instructions and the right size needles, they started for town.

Homer's Uncle Ulysses and Aunt Agnes have a very up-and-coming lunchroom over in Centerburg, just across from the court house on the town square. Uncle Ulysses is a man with advanced ideas and a weakness for labor-saving devices.

He equipped the lunchroom with automatic toasters, automatic coffee maker, automatic dishwasher, and an automatic doughnut maker. All just the latest thing in labor-saving devices.

Aunt Agnes would throw up her hands and sigh every time Uncle Ulysses bought a new labor-saving device. Sometimes she became unkindly disposed toward him for days and days. She was of the opinion that Uncle Ulysses just frittered away his spare time over at the barbershop with the sheriff and the boys, so, what was the good of a labor-saving device that gave you more time to fritter?

When Homer and his mother got to Centerburg, they stopped at the lunchroom, and after Aunt Agnes had come out and said, "My, how that boy does grow!" which was what she always said, she went off with Homer's mother in the car. Homer went into the lunchroom and said, "Howdy, Uncle Ulysses!"

"Oh, hello, Homer. You're just in time," said Uncle Ulysses. "I've been going over this automatic doughnut machine, oiling the machinery and cleaning the works . . . wonderful things, these labor-saving devices."

"Yep," agreed Homer, and he picked up a cloth and started polishing the metal trimmings while Uncle Ulysses tinkered with the inside workings.

"Opfwo-oof!!" sighed Uncle Ulysses and, "Look here, Homer, you've got a mechanical mind. See if you can find where these two pieces fit in. I'm going across to the barbershop for a spell, 'cause there's somethin' I've got to talk to the sheriff about. There won't be much business here until the double feature is over and I'll be back before then."

Then as Uncle Ulysses went out the door he said, "Uh, Homer, after you get the pieces in place, would you mind mixing up a batch of doughnut batter and putting it in the machine? You could turn the switch and make a few doughnuts to have on hand for the crowd after the movie . . . if you don't mind."

"O.K." said Homer, "I'll take care of everything."

A few minutes later a customer came in and said, "Good evening, Bud."

Homer looked up from putting the last piece in the doughnut machine and said, "Good evening, Sir, what can I do for you?"

"Well, young feller, I'd like a cup o' coffee and some doughnuts," said the customer.

"I'm sorry, Mister, but we won't have any doughnuts for about half an hour, until I can mix some dough and start this machine. I could give you some very fine sugar rolls instead."

"Well, Bud, I'm in no real hurry so I'll just have a cup o' coffee and wait around a bit for the doughnuts. Fresh doughnuts are always worth waiting for is what I always say."

"O.K.," said Homer, and he drew a cup of coffee from Uncle Ulysses' superautomatic coffee maker.

"Nice place you've got here," said the customer.

"Oh, yes," replied Homer, "this is a very up-and-coming lunchroom with all the latest improvements."

"Yes," said the stranger, "must be a good business. I'm in business too. A traveling man in outdoor advertising. I'm a sandwich man. Mr. Gabby's my name."

"My name is Homer. I'm glad to meet you, Mr. Gabby. It must be a fine profession, traveling and advertising sandwiches."

"Oh no," said Mr. Gabby, "I don't advertise sandwiches. I just wear any kind of an ad, one sign on front and one sign on behind, this way . . . Like a sandwich. Ya know what I mean?"

"Oh, I see. That must be fun, and you travel too?" asked Homer as he got out the flour and the baking powder.

"Yeah, I ride the rods between jobs, on freight trains, ya know what I mean?"

"Yes, but isn't that dangerous?" asked Homer.

"Of course there's a certain amount a risk, but you take any method a travel these days it's all dangerous. Ya know what I mean? Now take airplanes for instance . . ."

Just then a large shiny black car stopped in front of the lunchroom and a chauffeur helped a lady out of the rear door. They both came inside and the lady smiled at Homer and said, "We've stopped for a light snack. Some doughnuts and coffee would be simply marvelous."

Then Homer said, "I'm sorry, Ma'm, but the doughnuts won't be ready until I make this batter and start Uncle Ulysses' doughnut machine."

"Well now aren't *you* a clever young man to know how to make *doughnuts*!"

"Well," blushed Homer, "I've really never done it before, but I've got a recipe to follow."

"Now, young man, you simply must allow me to help. You know, I haven't made doughnuts for years, but I know the best recipe for doughnuts. It's marvelous, and we really must use it."

"But, Ma'm . . ." said Homer.

"Now just *wait* till you taste these doughnuts," said the lady. "Do you have an apron?" she asked, as she took off her fur coat and her rings and her jewelry and rolled up her sleeves. "Charles," she said to the chauffeur, "hand me that baking powder, that's right, and, young man, we'll need some nutmeg."

So Homer and the chauffeur stood by and handed things and cracked the eggs while the lady mixed and stirred. Mr. Gabby sat on his stool, sipped his coffee, and looked on with great interest.

"There!" said the lady when all of the ingredients were mixed. "Just *wait* till you taste these doughnuts!"

"It looks like an awful lot of batter," said Homer as he stood on a chair and poured it into the doughnut machine with the help of the chauffeur. "It's about *ten* times as much as Uncle Ulysses ever makes."

"But wait till you taste them!" said the lady with an eager look and a smile.

Homer got down from the chair and pushed a button on the machine marked, *Start*. Rings of batter started dropping into the hot fat. After a ring of batter was cooked on one side, an automatic gadget turned it over and the other side would cook. Then another automatic gadget gave the doughnut a little push and it rolled neatly down a little chute, all ready to eat.

"That's a simply *fascinating* machine," said the lady as she waited for the first doughnut to roll out.

"Here, young man, *you* must have the first one. Now isn't that just *too* delicious!? Isn't it simply marvelous?"

"Yes, Ma'm, it's very good," replied Homer as the lady handed doughnuts to Charles and to Mr. Gabby, and asked if they didn't think they were simply divine doughnuts.

"It's an old family recipe!" said the lady with pride.

Homer poured some coffee for the lady and her chauffeur and for Mr. Gabby, and a glass of milk for himself. Then they all sat down at the lunch counter to enjoy another few doughnuts apiece.

"I'm so glad you enjoy my doughnuts," said the lady. "But now, Charles, we really must be going. If you will just take this apron, Homer, and put two dozen doughnuts in a bag to take along, we'll be on our way. And, Charles, don't forget to pay the young man." She rolled down her sleeves and put on her jewelry; then Charles managed to get her into her big fur coat.

"Good night, young man, I haven't had so much fun in years. I *really* haven't," said the lady, as she went out the door and into the big shiny car.

"Those are sure good doughnuts," said Mr. Gabby as the car moved off.

"You bet!" said Homer. Then he and Mr. Gabby stood and watched the automatic doughnut machine make doughnuts.

After a few dozen more doughnuts had rolled down the little chute, Homer said, "I guess that's about enough doughnuts to sell to the aftertheater customers. I'd better turn the machine off for a while."

Homer pushed the button marked *Stop* and there was a little click, but nothing happened. The rings of batter kept right on dropping into the hot fat, and an automatic gadget kept right on turning them over, and another automatic gadget kept right on giving them a little push, and the doughnuts kept right on rolling down the little chute, all ready to eat.

"That's funny," said Homer, "I'm sure that's the right button!" He pushed it again but the automatic doughnut maker kept right on making doughnuts.

"Well I guess I must have put one of those pieces in backwards," said Homer.

"Then it might stop if you pushed the button marked *Start*," said Mr. Gabby.

Homer did, and the doughnuts still kept rolling down the little chute, just as regular as a clock can tick.

"I guess we could sell a few more doughnuts," said Homer, "but I'd better telephone Uncle Ulysses over at the barbershop." Homer gave the number, and while he waited for someone to answer he counted thirty-seven doughnuts roll down the little chute.

Finally someone answered "Hello! This is the sarberbhop, I mean the barbershop."

"Oh, hello, Sheriff. This is Homer. Could I speak to Uncle Ulysses?"

"Well, he's playing pinochle right now," said the sheriff. "Anythin' I can tell 'im?"

"Yes," said Homer. "I pushed the button marked *Stop* on the doughnut machine, but the rings of batter keep right on dropping into the hot fat, and an automatic gadget keeps right on turning them over, and another automatic gadget keeps giving them a little push, and the doughnuts keep right on rolling down the little chute! It won't stop!"

"O.K. Wold the hire, I mean, hold the wire and I'll tell 'im." Then Homer looked over his shoulder and counted another twenty-one doughnuts roll down the little chute, all ready to eat. Then the sheriff said, "He'll be right over . . . Just gotta finish this hand."

"That's good," said Homer. "G'by, Sheriff."

The window was full of doughnuts by now, so Homer and Mr. Gabby had to hustle around and start stacking them on plates and trays and lining them up on the counter.

"Sure are a lot of doughnuts!" said Homer.

"You bet!" said Mr. Gabby. "I lost count at twelve hundred and two, and that was quite a while back."

People had begun to gather outside the lunchroom window, and someone was saying, "There are almost as many doughnuts as there are people in Centerburg, and I wonder how in tarnation Ulysses thinks he can sell all of 'em!"

Every once in a while somebody would come inside and buy some, but while somebody bought two to eat and a dozen to take home, the machine made three dozen more.

By the time Uncle Ulysses and the sheriff arrived and pushed through the crowd the lunchroom was a calamity of doughnuts! Doughnuts in the window, doughnuts piled high on the shelves, doughnuts stacked on plates, doughnuts lined up twelve deep all along the counter, and doughnuts still rolling down the little chute, just as regular as a clock can tick.

"Hello, Sheriff, hello, Uncle Ulysses, we're having a little trouble here," said Homer.

"Well, I'll be dunked!!" said Uncle Ulysses.

"Dernd ef you won't be when Aggy gits home," said the sheriff.

"Mighty fine doughnuts though. What'll you do with 'em all, Ulysses?"

Uncle Ulysses groaned and said, "What will Aggy say? We'll never sell 'em all."

Then Mr. Gabby, who hadn't said anything for a long time, stopped piling doughnuts and said, "What you need is an advertising man. Ya know what I mean? You got the doughnuts, ya gotta create a market . . . Understand? . . . It's balancing the demand with the supply . . . That sort of thing."

"Yep!" said Homer. "Mr. Gabby's right. We have to enlarge our market. He's an advertising sandwich man, so if we hire him, he can walk up and down in front of the theater and get the customers."

"You're hired, Mr. Gabby!" said Uncle Ulysses.

Then everybody pitched in to paint the signs and to get Mr. Gabby sandwiched between. They painted "SALE ON DOUGHNUTS" in big letters on the window too.

Meanwhile the rings of batter kept right on dropping into the hot fat, and an automatic gadget kept right on turning them over, and another automatic gadget kept right on giving them a little push, and the doughnuts kept right on rolling down the little chute, just as regular as a clock can tick.

"I certainly hope this advertising works," said Uncle Ulysses, wagging his head. "Aggy'll certainly throw a fit if it don't."

The sheriff went outside to keep order, because there was quite a crowd by now—all looking at the doughnuts and guessing how many thousand there were, and watching new ones roll down the little chute, just as regular as a clock can tick. Homer and Uncle Ulysses kept stacking doughnuts. Once in a while somebody bought a few, but not very often.

Then Mr. Gabby came back and said, "Say, you know there's not much use o' me advertisin' at the theater. The show's all over, and besides almost everybody in town is out front watching that machine make doughnuts!"

"Zeus!" said Uncle Ulysses. "We must get rid of these doughnuts before Aggy gets here!"

"Looks like you will have ta hire a truck ta waul 'em ahay, I mean haul 'em away!!" said the sheriff, who had just come in. Just then there was a noise and a shoving out front, and the lady from the shiny black car and her chauffeur came pushing through the crowd and into the lunchroom.

"Oh, gracious!" she gasped, ignoring the doughnuts, "I've lost my diamond bracelet, and I know I left it here on the counter," she said, pointing to a place where the doughnuts were piled in stacks of two dozen.

"Yes, Ma'm, I guess you forgot it when you helped make the batter," said Homer.

Then they moved all the doughnuts around and looked for the diamond bracelet, but they couldn't find it anywhere. Meanwhile the doughnuts kept rolling down the little chute, just as regular as a clock can tick.

After they had looked all around, the sheriff cast a suspicious eye on Mr. Gabby, but Homer said, "He's all right, Sheriff, he didn't take it. He's a friend of mine."

Then the lady said, "I'll offer a reward of one hundred dollars for that bracelet! It really *must* be found! . . . it *really* must!"

"Now don't you worry, lady," said the sheriff. "I'll get your bracelet back!"

"Zeus! This is terrible!" said Uncle Ulysses. "First all of these doughnuts and then on top of all that, a lost diamond bracelet . . ."

Mr. Gabby tried to comfort him, and he said, "There's always a bright side. That machine'll probably run outta batter in an hour or two."

If Mr. Gabby hadn't been quick on his feet Uncle Ulysses would have knocked him down, sure as fate.

FRESH DOUGHNUTS
2 FOR 5¢
$ WHILE THEY LAST
$100.00 PRIZE
FOR FINDING
A BRACELET
INSIDE A DOUGHNUT
P.S. YOU HAVE TO GIVE THE
BRACELET BACK

Then while the lady wrung her hands and said, "We must find it we *must*!" and Uncle Ulysses was moaning about what Aunt Agnes would say, and the sheriff was eyeing Mr. Gabby, Homer sat down and thought hard.

Before twenty more doughnuts could roll down the little chute he shouted, "SAY! I know where the bracelet is! It was lying here on the counter and got mixed up in the batter by mistake! The bracelet is cooked inside one of these doughnuts!"

"Why . . . I really believe you're right," said the lady through her tears. "Isn't that *amazing*? Simply *amazing*!"

"I'll be durn'd!" said the sheriff.

"OhH-h!" moaned Uncle Ulysses. "Now we have to break up all of these doughnuts to find it. Think of the *pieces*! Think of the *crumbs*! Think of what *Aggy* will say!"

"Nope," said Homer. "We won't have to break them up. I've got a plan."

So Homer and the advertising man took some cardboard and some paint and printed another sign. They put this sign in the window, and the sandwich man wore two more signs that said the same thing and walked around in the crowd out front.

THEN . . . The doughnuts began to sell! *Everybody* wanted to buy doughnuts, *dozens* of doughnuts!

And that's not all. Everybody bought coffee to dunk the doughnuts in too. Those that didn't buy coffee bought milk or soda. It kept Homer and the lady and the chauffeur and Uncle Ulysses and the sheriff busy waiting on the people who wanted to buy doughnuts.

When all but the last couple of hundred doughnuts had been sold, Rupert Black shouted, "I GAWT IT!!" and sure enough . . . there was the diamond bracelet inside of his doughnut!

Then Rupert went home with a hundred dollars, the citizens of Centerburg went home full of doughnuts, the lady and her chauffeur drove off with the diamond bracelet, and Homer went home with his mother when she stopped by with Aunt Aggy.

As Homer went out of the door he heard Mr. Gabby say, "Neatest trick of merchandising I ever seen," and Aunt Aggy was looking skeptical while Uncle Ulysses was saying, "The rings of batter kept right on dropping into the hot fat, and the automatic gadget kept right on turning them over, and the other automatic gadget kept right on giving them a little push, and the doughnuts kept right on rolling down the little chute just as regular as a clock can tick—they just kept right on a-comin', an' a-comin', an' a-comin', an' a comin'."

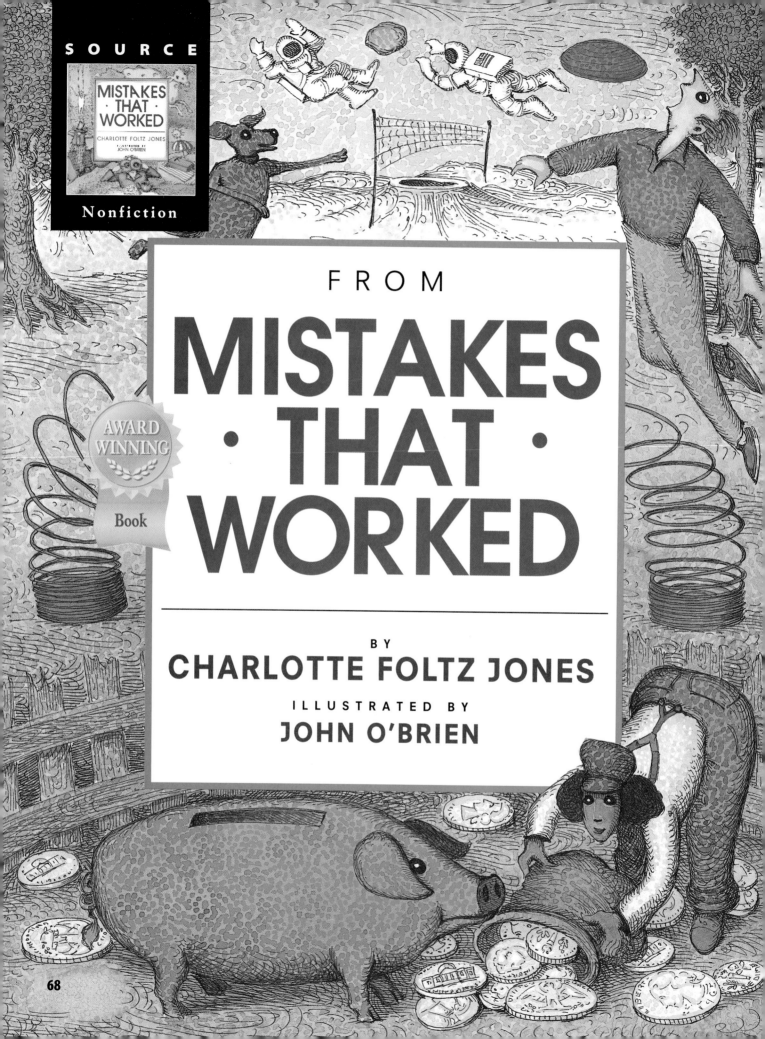

FROM

MISTAKES
· THAT ·
WORKED

BY

CHARLOTTE FOLTZ JONES

ILLUSTRATED BY

JOHN O'BRIEN

AWARD
WINNING

Book

Slinky

In 1943, during World War II, an engineer in the United States Navy was on a new ship's trial run. As he worked, a torsion spring suddenly fell to the floor. The spring flip-flopped as the ingenious man watched.

The naval engineer's name was Richard James, and when he returned home, he remembered the spring and the interesting way it flip-flopped. James and his wife Betty perfected a long steel ribbon tightly coiled into a spiral. They began production in 1945.

From that spring's accidental fall came a toy Americans have enjoyed for over forty years: the Slinky.

The nonelectrical, no-battery-required, nonvideo toy has fascinated three generations of children and adults alike. According to one estimate more than two million Slinkys have been sold and the only change in the original design has been to crimp the ends as a safety measure.

Betty James is now the company president and the Slinky is still hopping, skipping, jumping, and bouncing across floors and down stairs all over America.

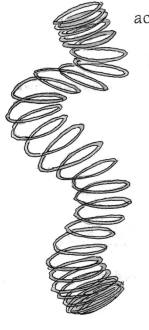

Piggy Bank

Dogs bury bones.

Squirrels gather nuts to last through the winter.

Camels store food and water so they can travel many days across deserts.

But do pigs save anything? No! Pigs save nothing. They bury nothing. They store nothing.

So why do we save our coins in a piggy bank? The answer: Because someone made a mistake.

During the Middle Ages, in about the fifteenth century, metal was expensive and seldom used for household wares. Instead, dishes and pots were made of an economical clay called pygg.

Whenever housewives could save an extra coin, they dropped it into one of their clay jars. They called this their pygg bank or their pyggy bank.

Over the next two hundred to three hundred years, people forgot that "pygg" referred to the earthenware material. In the nineteenth century when English potters received requests for pyggy banks, they produced banks shaped

like a pig. Of course, the pigs appealed to the customers and delighted children.

Pigs are still one of the most popular forms of coin banks sold in gift shops today.

Silly Putty

Sand.

There's lots of sand on Planet Earth. In fact, there's tons of it.

From sand, chemists can refine silicon. Plenty of silicon.

During World War II, the United States government needed a synthetic rubber for airplane tires, soldiers' boots, and other uses. Since silicon was so widely available, the government asked several large companies to have their engineers try to make a rubber substitute out of silicon.

In 1944 at General Electric, one of the engineers working on the silicon experiments was James Wright. One day while he was doing tests with silicon oil, he added boric acid. The result was a gooey substance that bounced.

Unfortunately, it had no apparent use. Samples were sent to engineers all over the world, but no one could find a use for it.

Then in 1949, four years after the war ended, a man named Peter Hodgson thought of an idea. After borrowing $147, he encased the goo in plastic "eggs" and renamed it "Silly Putty." Then he began selling it as a toy, first to adults and several years later to children.

It stretches. It bounces. When whacked with a hammer, it shatters. If it is pressed against newspaper comics, it will pick up the imprint. Silly Putty is truly amazing. It is now over forty years old, and was one of the first "fad" toys in America.

It has been used by athletes to strengthen their hand and forearm muscles. It can level the leg of a wiggly table or clean typewriter keys. It removes lint from clothes and animal hair from furniture.

The astronauts on the *Apollo 8* spacecraft played with Silly Putty when they got bored, and they used it to keep tools from floating around after they left the Earth's gravity.

It was used by the Columbus Zoo in Ohio in 1981 to take hand and foot prints of gorillas.

It's the toy with only one moving part, and best of all, Silly Putty is still priced so almost everyone can afford it.

The Frisbee Disc

The Frisbee was invented 2,700 years ago.

Well . . . not really!

Discus throwing was a part of the early Olympic games in Greece 2,700 years ago. And the design of the Frisbee disc is similar to the discus thrown in the Olympic games. But the Frisbee is a Frisbee, not a discus. And its invention was *not* the result of some inventor staying up nights.

The original Frisbee was spelled Frisbie and it was metal. It was not invented to be thrown — except into an oven. It was a pie tin stamped with the words "Frisbie Pies" since the pies came from the Frisbie Bakery in Bridgeport, Connecticut.

The Frisbie pie tins would probably have done nothing more than hold pies if it hadn't been for some Yale University students. The Yale students bought Frisbie pies and once the pie was eaten, they began tossing the tins to each other. They would call out, "Frisbie!" to the person to whom they were tossing the pan, or to warn people walking nearby to watch for the flying objects.

And so, intending simply to toss a pie tin back and forth, the Yale University students invented what has grown into the Frisbee we know today.

Walter F. Morrison produced the first plastic models. The Wham-O Manufacturing Company of San Gabriel, California, began manufacturing Frisbee discs in the mid-1950s and since 1957 has made sixteen models. Now about thirty companies make flying discs.

There are flying disc clubs, tournaments, champions, a world association, and a publication just for flying disc enthusiasts. The National Frisbee Disc Festival is held each September.

The *Guinness Book of World Records* reports that the record time for keeping a flying disc aloft was set by Don Cain on May 26, 1984, when he kept one in the air for 16.72 seconds.

Disc play is good exercise. It's fun. It's easy, yet challenging. It doesn't cost much. And, best of all, it's a sport you can enjoy with your favorite dog!

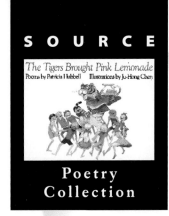
from
The Tigers Brought Pink Lemonade
by *Patricia Hubbell*
illustration by *Ju-Hong Chen*

THE INVENTOR THINKS UP HELICOPTERS

"Why not
a
vertical
whirling
winding
bug,
that hops like a cricket
crossing a rug,
that swerves like a dragonfly
testing his steering,
twisting and veering?
Fleet as a beetle.
Up
down
left
right,
jounce, bounce, day and night.
It could land in a pasture the size of a dot . . .
Why not?"

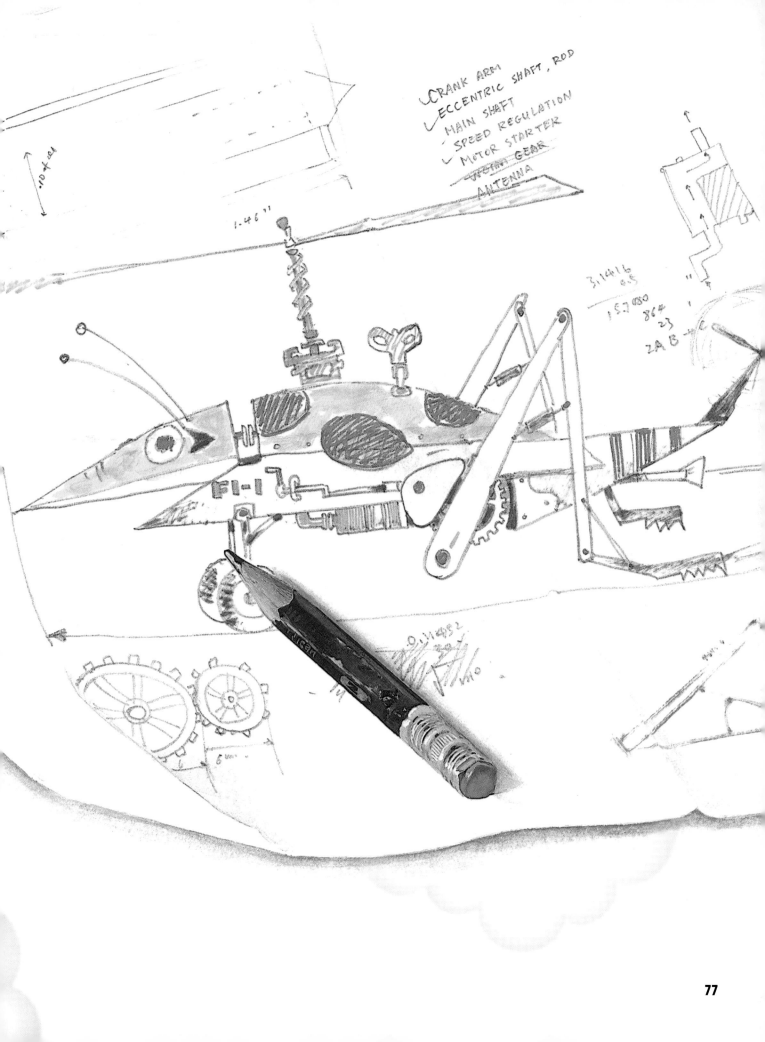

CRANK ARM
ECCENTRIC SHAFT, ROD
MAIN SHAFT
SPEED REGULATION
MOTOR STARTER
WORM GEAR
ANTENNA

FI-1

How to

Make an Invention Diagram

Have you ever had an idea for an invention? Did you ever look at an everyday object and think, "I could improve that?" Inventors often write down their ideas when they think of them. Later, they may decide to develop an idea by making a diagram of it.

What is an invention diagram? An invention diagram is a drawing of an invention with each of its parts labeled, and a list of materials needed to make it. The diagram includes a description of what the invention can do.

Nathan Matter:
The Handy Helper

flexible magnet

velcro fastens it to wrist

magnetic bracelet
holds nails and tacks

● **The name of the inventor**

● **The name of the invention**

Matthew McCurdy's
Crayons for Keeps

long bolt

handle pushes crayon out

hard nylon dowel

crayon

protects crayons from breaking

Clearly labeled parts

Description of the invention's function

1 Make a List

Jot down ideas for inventions or product improvements that you would like to see. Don't worry if your ideas seem silly—how about motorized sneakers, or sunglasses with a built-in video camera? Write down as many ideas as you can.

TOOLS

- pencil, paper, ruler
- colored markers

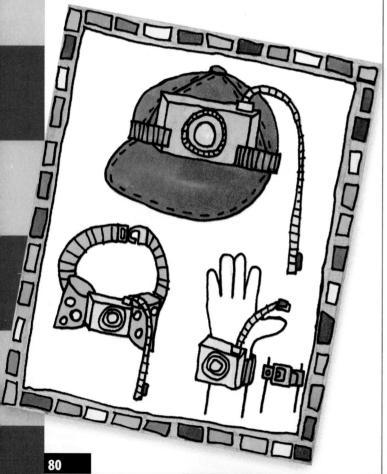

2 Design Your Invention

Look over your ideas and choose the one you like best. Think of different ways to design your invention. For example, if your invention is a talking watch, one design idea might include a talking cartoon head on the watch. A different design idea would be a digital watch that would announce the time and date every hour. Write down at least three different design ideas for your invention.

3 Draw a Diagram

Pick your favorite design idea and make a diagram of it. You may want to draw a picture of the whole thing and then a closeup of one of its important parts. Or you could show what your invention looks like on both the outside and the inside. Be sure to label each part of your invention. Underneath the diagram, list the materials you would need to build it.

Tip Make some quick sketches of your invention before you draw your finished diagram.

4 Add Finishing Touches

Write a brief description of what your invention does. Don't forget to name it. Share your invention diagram with your classmates.

If You Are Using a Computer . . .

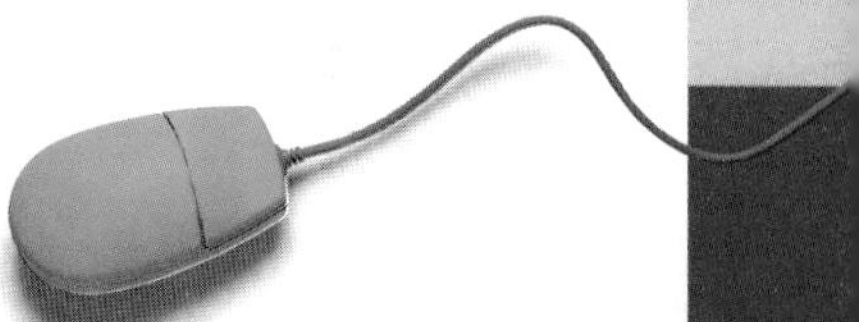

Keep track of your invention ideas by typing them in the journal format. You also can experiment with font sizes and styles to make labels for your diagram.

THINK

Why is a diagram an important step in the process of developing an invention?

Julie Lewis
Inventor ▶

PASSENGER TRAIN TRAVELLING ON SOUND WAVES

ROBOTIC VACUUM CLEANER

SOLAR-POWERED SPACECRAFT

REMOTE CONTROLLED ROBOT SURGEON

HEART

ROBO VAC

FLOATING AIR-AUTO

COMPUTERIZED WAITER

MORE H₂O, SIR?

SURE!

MENU

MORE WATER?

ULTRAVIOLET RAY PROTECTOR

Fast Forward

Share Kate's excitement as she talks to a space alien on her dad's computer. Then marvel at the size of the first computer ever built.

Step into a time machine with Angela and zip into the future. Next, learn about inventions that may really exist in the future.

PROJECT

Choose the best way to market your invention.

from
The Computer Nut

The Star Ship

by

Betsy Byars

illustrated by

Lisa Adams

Kate, who's a computer nut, receives a mysterious message while drawing a self-portrait on her father's computer. She waits impatiently for another chance to make contact with the stranger who sent the message.

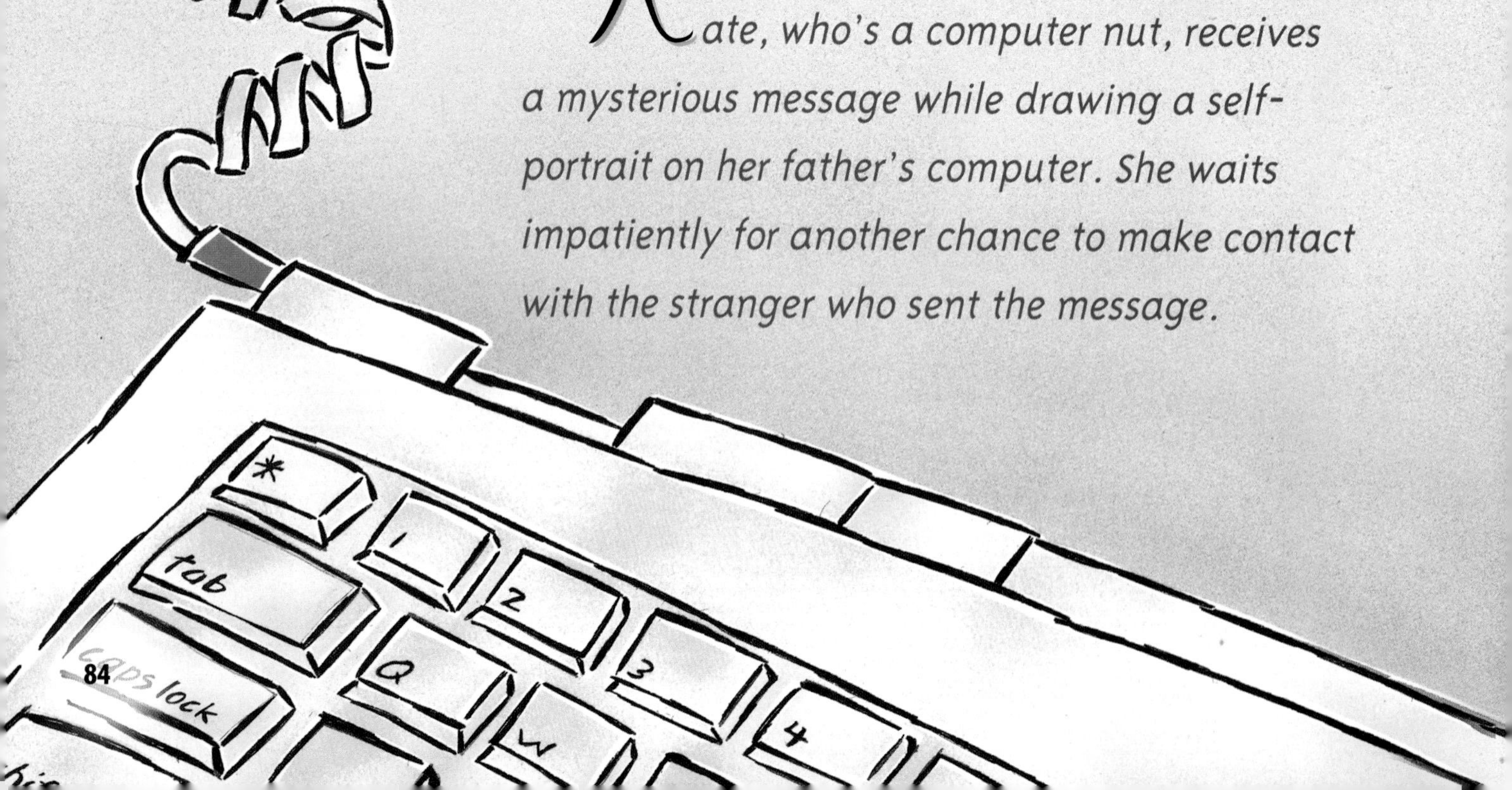

It was Saturday morning, and rain had been coming down for three hours, a cold, solid October rain that brought winter closer.

Kate came into her father's office, shaking rain from her slicker. She threw back her hood and crossed to the door to the computer room. "It is pouring," she said to Miss Markham.

"I'm surprised your mother let you out on a day like this."

"She almost didn't. She said, 'Just because your father is a doctor is no reason to take chances with your health . . . blah . . . blah . . . blah.' And I said, 'I never take chances with my health because when I get sick I have to take free samples.'"

"Kate!"

"That's what my mother said. 'Kate!' Anyway, it's true. I have never had drugstore medicine in my life. How much longer are you going to be?"

"Until I finish the bills."

"But that'll be hours!"

"Well, I'm going to take a break in five minutes. How about that?"

"That's better."

Kate walked to the window. She looked out at the rainswept street. She closed the blinds, opened them to the same scene, closed them.

"What is wrong with you?" Miss Markham asked without looking around. "Why are you so restless?"

"I'm not restless. I just want to know who sent me that message. And I would like to find out before Linda completely ruins me. Yesterday she—" Kate broke off.

"She what?"

"Nothing."

Kate opened the blinds again. The memory of being pushed into Frank Wilkins, of leaving a slice of pizza on his back, had been returning like an echo to embarrass her again and again. Even now her cheeks reddened. She turned from the window with a sigh.

"Okay, okay, the computer is yours. I need to make some phone calls anyway. Mrs. Brown thinks Arthur swallowed some of the dog's worm pills." She slipped out the accounting program. "I'll be back in twenty minutes, Kate."

Kate slid into the chair as Miss Markham got up. She took a deep breath and exhaled. Before Miss Markham was out of the room, she had begun to type.

THIS IS THE COMPUTER NUT. DOES SOMEBODY OUT THERE HAVE A MESSAGE FOR ME?

She waited, watching the screen. She moistened her dry lips. She typed again.

REPEAT. THIS IS THE COMPUTER NUT. IS THERE A MESSAGE FOR ME?

She waited. When nothing happened, she gave a mock scream of impatience.

"Give it a chance," Miss Markham called from her desk.

"I *hate* to wait for anything. You know that." Kate turned back to the video screen. She drummed her fingers on the desk. "I just *hate* to—"

Suddenly Kate straightened. Words were appearing on the screen.

COMPUTER NUT, THAT IS AFFIRMATIVE. THIS IS BB-9 AND I WAS TRYING TO CONTACT YOU.

"BB-9?" Kate asked herself. "I wonder what that stands for—some sort of program?"
She typed:

I AM UNFAMILIAR WITH BB-9. WHAT DOES THAT STAND FOR?

The answer came at once:

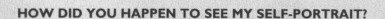

BB-9 IS A SHORTENED VERSION OF MY DESIGNATION. MY FULL DESIGNATION IS BB-947-82-A-1070-BLX-09. THAT IS A CODE THAT WOULD HAVE NO MEANING TO YOU AT THIS TIME. LET ME SAY THAT YOU ARE IN CONTACT WITH A PEACEABLE BEING WITHOUT MALICE OF INTENT WHOSE INTEREST IS IN MUTUAL EXCHANGE OF INFORMATION.

Kate paused. Suddenly she wished Linda were there with her to laugh, to wonder at the real identity of BB-9, to yell, "I know who it is, Kate!" She swallowed and typed:

HOW DID YOU HAPPEN TO SEE MY SELF-PORTRAIT?

She waited.

I SAW IT ON MY MASTER CONSOLE WHICH MONITORS ALL TERRESTRIAL TERMINALS. YOUR SELF-PORTRAIT WAS THE ONLY INTERESTING THING ON THE MASTER CONSOLE AT 16:39 THURSDAY. ALSO YOU LOOKED AS IF YOU HAD A SENSE OF HUMOR, AS IF YOU WOULD ENJOY A GOOD LAUGH. THAT IS WHY I DECIDED TO CONTACT YOU.

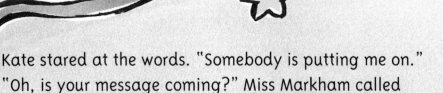

Kate stared at the words. "Somebody is putting me on."

"Oh, is your message coming?" Miss Markham called from the outer office.

"*Something's* coming."

"Well, tell me about it when you get through."

Kate let out her breath between her teeth, then typed:

WHERE, EXACTLY, IS THIS MASTER CONSOLE? HOW FAR AWAY?

She put one hand under her chin and watched the screen. "Well?"

THE MASTER CONSOLE IS 2591.82 MILES DIRECTLY ABOVE YOU AT THIS MOMENT, MOVING IN A GEOSYNCHRONOUS ORBIT.

"Oh, come on. You expect me to believe that?" Kate put her hands on the keyboard.

WHAT ARE YOU? A SATELLITE? A—

"I'm ready to use the computer now, Kate," Miss Markham called.

"I'm almost through."

The answer was coming. Kate leaned forward.

NO SATELLITE, COMPUTER NUT. I AM IN A SELF-CONTAINED UNIT, A STAR SHIP, AS YOU EARTHLINGS WOULD SAY, AND I HAVE BEEN MONITORING EARTH'S COMPUTERS IN PREPARATION FOR AN OCTOBER LANDING.

Kate snorted with disgust. "An October landing. Who does he think he is? E.T.?"

AND JUST HOW, WHEN, AND WHERE ARE YOU GOING TO MAKE THIS LANDING?

She waited, leaning forward on her elbows.

THE ACTUAL DETAILS OF MY LANDING CANNOT BE REVEALED AT THIS TIME. HOWEVER, I WOULD BE GLAD TO DEPICT MY SPACE TRANSPORT. IT IS NOT AN UNUSUAL VEHICLE—MUCH LIKE OTHERS THAT HAVE COME TO YOUR PLANET—BUT IF IT WOULD BE OF INTEREST TO YOU . . .

Kate typed:

IT WOULD DEFINITELY BE OF INTEREST.

"Kate, are you finished?" Miss Markham called.

"Just let me see this spaceship," Kate called back.

"Spaceship?"

"Yes, some nut is pretending to be from outer space, and he is going to draw his spaceship. It's nothing out of the ordinary, just some little vehicle he's been tooling around the galaxy in."

"This I gotta see."

Miss Markham came into the room and stood behind Kate. They watched the screen as lines began to appear. For a moment there was not a sound in the office.

Then, when the picture was finished, Miss Markham let out her breath in a low whistle. "Well," she said, "as space vehicles go, that is not bad."

Kate slapped her hands down on the desk. "I hate it when people try to put me on. I *hate* it."

"Don't be so intense, hon. You take life too seriously. It's just somebody playing a joke on you. Go along with it. Ask him to send a picture of himself, of his planet."

Kate kept staring at the spaceship until the picture disappeared and words replaced it on the screen.

**WHAT DID YOU THINK OF MY SPACESHIP, COMPUTER NUT?
WAS IT A DISAPPOINTMENT? WAS IT AS YOU EXPECTED?**

"Tell him, 'Yes.' Tell him you'd like to go for a ride. Tell him you'll meet him out in front of the office. Ask him if he's got an alien friend for me." Miss Markham broke off and let her hands drop onto Kate's shoulders. "I am getting carried away. Whatever you tell him will have to be some other time. I need the computer now."

Kate typed:

COMPUTER NUT LOGGING.

"There." Kate got up and walked to the window. She stared out at the wet street.

"You'll find out who it is," Miss Markham said.

Kate flicked her hair behind her ears. "I'm beginning to wonder," she said.

Kate does finally discover the identity of BB-9, the mysterious message sender. And is he ever out of this world!

93

SOURCE

SCHOLASTIC NEWS®

News Magazine

The First Computers

A History Play by
Richard Chevat

Illustrated by
Dan Picasso

Fast forward to a TV newsroom of the future where a reporter can travel back to 1943 to cover the unveiling of a new invention.

Sue Smith

Gary Granite

Grace Hopper

Howard Aiken

Mary Roberts

one of the first computer programmers. Wait a minute, I think I see her now! Oh, Ms. Hopper! Excuse me, I'm Sue Smith from Time-Travel News. Could you answer some questions for our viewers?

Hopper: Sure, but we'll have to hurry. I'm very busy.

Smith: All right. First, could you show us the machine that you are working on?

Hopper: Show you . . . ? That's it right there!

Smith: That's a computer? It must be fifty feet long!

Hopper: Fifty-one, to be exact. It's also eight feet tall and two feet thick and weighs about five tons. Come on, let's go inside.

Smith: Inside? OK, if you say so. Gary, I don't know if you can see this, but Grace Hopper is taking me *inside* the computer.

Granite: Great, I always wanted to know where those little space aliens went when they weren't attacking my planet.

Hopper: This is the inside of the Mark 1 computer. It is powered by a small electric motor which turns this shaft here.

Granite: Hello, this is Gary Granite in the newsroom. Our time-traveling reporter, Sue Smith, has traveled back to the year 1943 to get a first-hand look at one of the first computers. Sue, can you hear me?

Smith: Yes, Gary. I am at Harvard University, in Cambridge, Massachusetts. Right here in this room, one of the first modern computers is being put together.

Granite: Hey, that sounds neat! Can you get an interview with the first person to play Pac Man?

Smith: No, Gary, I'm here to talk to Grace Hopper, who was

Smith: It looks like some kind of engine.

Hopper: Yes, sort of. As you can see, it is mainly mechanical, that is, it works with moving parts.

Granite: Sue, ask her where the microchips are.

Smith: Gary, microchips won't be invented until 1958.

Hopper: What won't be invented until 1958? Say, who did you say you are?

Smith: Uh, never mind. Could you explain what all these rolls of paper are for?

Hopper: The instructions for running this machine are written on this paper tape. Actually, they're not really written. Instead, it's a code of small holes punched in the paper.

Smith: That's the program?

Hopper: Yes, that would be another name for the instructions—a program.

Smith: Tell us, what can the Mark 1 do?

Hopper: Why don't you ask my boss, Howard Aiken? The Mark 1 is his invention.

Aiken: Did someone mention my name?

Smith: Mr. Aiken, could you explain what the Mark 1 will do when it is finished?

Aiken: Well, the Mark 1 is really a big calculating machine. It will be able to perform large numbers of calculations in a short time. The Navy is paying part of our costs. They plan to use the Mark 1 to help win World War II.

Smith: Can you give us an example?

Roberts: I can.

Smith: Who are you?

Roberts: My name is Mary Roberts, and I work for the Navy. There are 30 women who work in my office. Sometimes it takes all of us working four or five days to solve just one problem.

Aiken: Yes, you see, they have to use old-fashioned adding machines and pencils and paper. But the Mark 1 will be able to do the same amount of work in just a few hours.

Smith: So in some ways, the Mark 1 is like a giant adding machine?

Aiken: You could say that. But it can handle problems that are much more complex than any adding machine.

Hopper: Of course, the Mark 1 is just the beginning. Our goal is to build a machine that can handle many different problems and work even faster than Mark 1.

Smith: A computer.

Hopper: That's one name for it. We think these new machines will be a great aid to science.

Granite: Not to mention video games.

Hopper: What did you say?

Smith: Uh, nothing.

Hopper: Well, we have a lot of work to do.

Smith: I guess you're still getting all of the bugs out of the system.

▲ **The actual Mark 1 computer unveiled in 1943**

Hopper: Oh, you heard about that, did you?

Smith: Heard about what?

Hopper: Our bug. I have it right here, taped to this piece of paper.

Smith: That's a moth!

Aiken: We were having problems with the computer, and no one could figure out what was wrong. Then Grace found this in the machine. It was stuck in one of the relay switches.

Smith: You don't mean . . . ?

Hopper: Yes, this is the very first computer bug.

Smith: Well, this certainly is historic.

Hopper: Yes, well, we really have to get back to work.

Aiken: Yes, we were in the middle of a major problem.

Granite: Sue, maybe you should loan them your computer.

Hopper: You have a computer?

Smith: Yes, I, uh, that is . . .

Hopper: Is it close by?

Smith: Well actually, it's, that is . . . you're looking at it. It's right here on my wrist.

Hopper: Hey, who did you say you are?

Smith: Uh, this is Sue Smith, of Time-Travel News, signing off.

Aiken: Did she say on her wrist?

Roberts: She must have a very strong arm.

Hopper: I thought there was something strange about her.

SOURCE

Short Story Collection

from

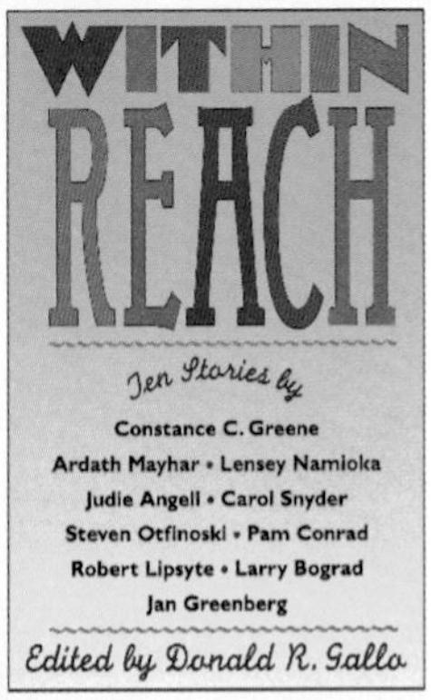

WITHIN REACH

edited by Donald R. Gallo

LAFFF

AWARD WINNING Author

by Lensey Namioka

illustrated by Tim Lee

In movies, geniuses have frizzy white hair, right? They wear thick glasses and have names like Dr. Zweistein.

Peter Lu didn't have frizzy white hair. He had straight hair, as black as licorice. He didn't wear thick glasses, either, since his vision was normal.

Peter's family, like ours, had immigrated from China, but they had settled here first. When we moved into a house just two doors down from the Lus, they gave us some good advice on how to get along in America.

I went to the same school as Peter, and we walked to the school bus together every morning. Like many Chinese parents, mine made sure that I worked very hard in school.

In spite of all I could do, my grades were nothing compared to Peter's. He was at the top in all his classes. We walked to the school bus without talking because I was a little scared of him. Besides, he was always deep in thought.

Peter didn't have any friends. Most of the kids thought he was a nerd because they saw his head always buried in books. I didn't think he even tried to join the rest of us or cared what the others thought of him.

Then on Halloween he surprised us all. As I went down the block trick-or-treating, dressed as a zucchini in my green sweats, I heard a strange, deep voice behind me say, "How do you do."

I yelped and turned around. Peter was wearing a long, black Chinese gown with slits in the sides. On his head he had a little round cap, and down each side of his mouth drooped a thin, long mustache.

"I am Dr. Lu Manchu, the mad scientist," he announced, putting his hands in his sleeves and bowing.

He smiled when he saw me staring at his costume. I smiled back. I knew he was making fun of the way some kids believed in stereotypes about Chinese people. Still, his was a scary smile, somehow.

Some of the other kids came up, and when they saw Peter, they were impressed. "Hey, neat!" said one boy.

I hadn't expected Peter to put on a costume and go trick-or-treating like a normal kid. So maybe he did want to join the others after all—at least some of the time. After that night he wasn't a nerd anymore. He was Dr. Lu. Even some of the teachers began to call him that.

When we became too old for trick-or-treating, Peter was still Dr. Lu Manchu. The rumor was that he was working on a fantastic machine in his parents' garage. But nobody had any idea what it was.

One evening, as I was coming home from a baby-sitting job, I cut across the Lus' backyard. Passing their garage, I saw through a little window that the light was on. My curiosity got the better of me, and I peeked in.

I saw a booth that looked like a shower stall. A stool stood in the middle of the stall, and hanging over the stool was something that looked like a great big shower head.

Suddenly a deep voice behind me said, "Good evening, Angela." Peter bowed and smiled his scary smile.

"What are you doing?" I squeaked.

Still in his strange, deep voice, Peter said, "What are *you* doing? After all, this is my garage."

"I was just cutting across your yard to get home. Your parents never complained before."

"I thought you were spying on me." said Peter. "I thought you wanted to know about my machine." He hissed when he said the word *machine*.

Honestly, he was beginning to frighten me. "What machine?" I demanded. "You mean this shower-stall thing?"

He drew himself up and narrowed his eyes, making them into thin slits. "This is my time machine!"

I goggled at him. "You mean . . . you mean . . . this machine can send you forward and backward in time?"

"Well, actually, I can only send things forward in time," admitted Peter, speaking in his normal voice again. "That's why I'm calling the machine LAFFF. It stands for Lu's Artifact For Fast Forward."

Of course Peter always won first prize at the annual statewide science fair. But that's a long way from making a time machine. Minus his mustache and long Chinese gown, he was just Peter Lu.

"I don't believe it!" I said. "I bet LAFFF is only good for a laugh."

"Okay, Angela. I'll show you!" hissed Peter.

He sat down on the stool and twisted a dial. I heard some *bleeps*, *cheeps*, and *gurgles*. Peter disappeared.

He must have done it with mirrors. I looked around the garage. I peeked under the tool bench. There was no sign of him.

"Okay, I give up," I told him. "It's a good trick, Peter. You can come out now."

Bleep, *cheep*, and *gurgle* went the machine, and there was Peter, sitting on the stool. He held a red rose in his hand. "What do you think of that?"

I blinked. "So you produced a flower. Maybe you had it under the stool."

"Roses bloom in June, right?" he demanded.

That was true. And this was December.

"I sent myself forward in time to June when the flowers were blooming," said Peter. "And I picked the rose from our yard. Convinced, Angela?"

It was too hard to swallow. "You said you couldn't send things back in time," I objected. "So how did you bring the rose back?"

But even as I spoke I saw that his hands were empty. The rose was gone.

"That's one of the problems with the machine," said Peter. "When I send myself forward, I can't seem to stay there for long. I snap back to my own time after only a minute. Anything I bring with me snaps back to its own time, too. So my rose has gone back to this June."

I was finally convinced, and I began to see possibilities. "Wow, just think: If I don't want to do the dishes, I can send myself forward to the time when the dishes are already done."

"That won't do you much good," said Peter. "You'd soon pop back to the time when the dishes were still dirty."

Too bad. "There must be something your machine is good for," I said. Then I had another idea. "Hey, you can bring me back a piece of fudge from the future, and I can eat it twice: once now, and again in the future."

"Yes, but the fudge wouldn't stay in your stomach," said Peter. "It would go back to the future."

"That's even better!" I said. "I can enjoy eating the fudge over and over again without getting fat!"

It was late, and I had to go home before my parents started to worry. Before I left, Peter said, "Look, Angela, there's still a lot of work to do on LAFFF. Please don't tell anybody about the machine until I've got it right."

A few days later I asked him how he was doing.

"I can stay in the future time a bit longer now," he said. "Once I got it up to four minutes."

"Is that enough time to bring me back some fudge from the future?" I asked.

"We don't keep many sweets around the house," he said. "But I'll see what I can do."

A few minutes later, he came back with a spring roll for me. "My mother was frying these in the kitchen, and I snatched one while she wasn't looking."

I bit into the hot, crunchy spring roll, but before I finished chewing, it disappeared. The taste of soy sauce, green onions, and bean sprouts stayed a little longer in my mouth, though.

It was fun to play around with LAFFF, but it wasn't really useful. I didn't know what a great help it would turn out to be.

Every year our school held a writing contest, and the winning story for each grade got printed in our school magazine. I wanted desperately to win. I worked awfully hard in school, but my parents still thought I could do better.

Winning the writing contest would show my parents that I was really good in something. I love writing stories, and I have lots of ideas. But when I actually write them down, my stories never turn out as good as I thought. I just can't seem to find the right words, because English isn't my first language.

I got an honorable mention last year, but it wasn't the same as winning and showing my parents my name, Angela Tang, printed in the school magazine.

The deadline for the contest was getting close, and I had a pile of stories written, but none of them looked like a winner.

Then, the day before the deadline, *boing*, a brilliant idea hit me.

I thought of Peter and his LAFFF machine.

I rushed over to the Lus' garage and, just as I had hoped, Peter was there, tinkering with his machine.

"I've got this great idea for winning the story contest," I told him breathlessly. "You see, to be certain of winning, I have to write the story that would be the winner."

"That's obvious," Peter said dryly. "In fact, you're going around in a circle."

"Wait, listen!" I said. "I want to use LAFFF and go forward to the time when the next issue of the school magazine is out. Then I can read the winning story."

After a moment Peter nodded. "I see. You plan to write down the winning story after you've read it and then send it in to the contest."

I nodded eagerly. "The story would *have* to win, because it's the winner!"

Peter began to look interested. "I've got LAFFF to the point where I can stay in the future for seven minutes now. Will that be long enough for you?"

"I'll just have to work quickly," I said.

Peter smiled. It wasn't his scary Lu Manchu smile, but a nice smile. He was getting as excited as I was. "Okay, Angela. Let's go for it."

He led me to the stool. "What's your destination?" he asked. "I mean, *when's* your destination?"

Suddenly I was nervous. I told myself that Peter had made many time trips, and he looked perfectly healthy.

Why not? What have I got to lose—except time?

I took a deep breath. "I want to go forward three weeks in time." By then I'd have a copy of the new school magazine in my room.

"Ready, Angela?" asked Peter.

"As ready as I'll ever be," I whispered.

Bleep, *cheep*, and *gurgle*. Suddenly Peter disappeared.

What went wrong? Did Peter get sent by mistake, instead of me?

Then I realized what had happened. Three weeks later in time Peter might be somewhere else. No wonder I couldn't see him.

There was no time to be lost. Rushing out of Peter's garage, I ran over to our house and entered through the back door.

Mother was in the kitchen. When she saw me, she stared. "Angela! I thought you were upstairs taking a shower!"

"Sorry!" I panted. "No time to talk!"

I dashed up to my room. Then I suddenly had a strange idea. What if I met *myself* in my room? Argh! It was a spooky thought.

There was nobody in my room. Where was I? I mean, where was the I of three weeks later?

Wait. Mother had just said she thought I was taking a shower. Down the hall, I could hear the water running in the bathroom. Okay. That meant I wouldn't run into me for a while.

I went to the shelf above my desk and frantically pawed through the junk piled there. I found it! I found the latest issue of the school magazine, the one with the winning stories printed in it.

How much time had passed? Better hurry.

The shower had stopped running. This meant the other me was out of the bathroom. Have to get out of here!

Too late. Just as I started down the stairs, I heard Mother talking again. "Angela! A minute ago you were all dressed! Now you're in your robe again and your hair's all wet! I don't understand."

I shivered. It was scary, listening to Mother talking to myself downstairs. I heard my other self answering something, then the sound of her—my—steps coming up the stairs. In a panic, I dodged into the spare room and closed the door.

I heard the steps—my steps—go past and into my room.

The minute I heard the door of my room close, I rushed out and down the stairs.

Mother was standing at the foot of the stairs. When she saw me, her mouth dropped. "But . . . but . . . just a minute ago you were in your robe and your hair was all wet!"

"See you later, Mother," I panted. And I ran.

Behind me I heard Mother muttering, "I'm going mad!"

I didn't stop and try to explain. I might go mad, too.

It would be great if I could just keep the magazine with me. But, like the spring roll, it would get carried back to its own time after a few minutes. So the next best thing was to read the magazine as fast as I could.

It was hard to run and flip through the magazine at the same time. But I made it back to Peter's garage and plopped down on the stool.

At last I found the story: the story that had won the contest in our grade. I started to read.

Suddenly I heard *bleep*, *cheep*, and *gurgle*, and Peter loomed up in front of me. I was back in my original time again.

But I still had the magazine! Now I had to read the story before the magazine popped back to the future. It was hard to concentrate with Peter jumping up and down impatiently, so different from his usual calm, collected self.

I read a few paragraphs, and I was beginning to see how the story would shape up. But before I got any further, the magazine disappeared from my hand.

So I didn't finish reading the story. I didn't reach the end, where the name of the winning writer was printed.

That night I stayed up very late to write down what I remembered of the story. It had a neat plot, and I could see why it was the winner.

I hadn't read the entire story, so I had to make up the ending myself. But that was okay, since I knew how it should come out.

The winners of the writing contest would be announced at the school assembly on Friday. After we had filed into the assembly hall and sat down, the principal gave a speech. I tried not to fidget while he explained about the contest.

Suddenly I was struck by a dreadful thought. Somebody in my class had written the winning story, the one I had copied. Wouldn't that person be declared the winner, instead of me?

The principal started announcing the winners. I chewed my knuckles in an agony of suspense, as I waited to see who would be announced as the winner in my class. Slowly, the principal began with the lowest grade. Each winner walked in slow motion to the stage, while the principal slowly explained why the story was good.

At last, at last, he came to our grade. "The winner is . . ." He stopped, slowly got out his handkerchief, and slowly blew his nose. Then he cleared his throat. "The winning story is 'Around and Around,' by Angela Tang."

I sat like a stone, unable to move. Peter nudged me. "Go on, Angela! They're waiting for you."

I got up and walked up to the stage in a daze. The principal's voice seemed to be coming from far, far away as he told the audience that I had written a science fiction story about time travel.

The winners each got a notebook bound in imitation leather for writing more stories. Inside the cover of the notebook was a ballpoint pen. But the best prize was having my story in the school magazine with my name printed at the end.

Then why didn't I feel good about winning?

After assembly, the kids in our class crowded around to congratulate me. Peter formally shook my hand. "Good work, Angela," he said, and winked at me.

That didn't make me feel any better. I hadn't won the contest fairly. Instead of writing the story myself, I had copied it from the school magazine.

That meant someone in our class—one of the kids here—had actually written the story. Who was it?

My heart was knocking against my ribs as I stood there and waited for someone to complain that I had stolen his story.

Nobody did.

As we were riding the school bus home, Peter looked at me. "You don't seem very happy about winning the contest, Angela."

"No, I'm not," I mumbled. "I feel just awful."

"Tell you what," suggested Peter. "Come over to my house and we'll discuss it."

"What is there to discuss?" I asked glumly. "I won the contest because I cheated."

"Come on over, anyway. My mother bought a fresh package of humbow in Chinatown."

I couldn't turn down that invitation. Humbow, a roll stuffed with barbecued pork, is my favorite snack.

Peter's mother came into the kitchen while we were munching, and he told her about the contest.

Mrs. Lu looked pleased. "I'm very glad, Angela. You have a terrific imagination, and you deserve to win."

"I like Angela's stories," said Peter. "They're original."

It was the first compliment he had ever paid me, and I felt my face turning red.

After Mrs. Lu left us, Peter and I each had another humbow. But I was still miserable. "I wish I had never started this. I feel like such a jerk."

Peter looked at me, and I swear he was enjoying himself. "If you stole another student's story, why didn't that person complain?"

"I don't know!" I wailed.

"Think!" said Peter. "You're smart, Angela. Come on, figure it out."

Me, smart? I was so overcome to hear myself called smart by a genius like Peter that I just stared at him.

He had to repeat himself. "Figure it out, Angela!"

I tried to concentrate. Why was Peter looking so amused?

The light finally dawned. "Got it," I said slowly. "*I'm* the one who wrote the story."

"The winning story is your own, Angela, because that's the one that won."

My head began to go around and around. "But where did the original idea for the story come from?"

"What made the plot so good?" asked Peter. His voice sounded unsteady.

"Well, in my story, my character used a time machine to go forward in time . . ."

"Okay, whose idea was it to use a time machine?"

"It was mine," I said slowly. I remembered the moment when the idea had hit me with a *boing*.

"So you s-stole f-from yourself!" sputtered Peter. He started to roar with laughter. I had never seen him break down like that. At this rate, he might wind up being human.

When he could talk again, he asked me to read my story to him.

I began. " 'In movies, geniuses have frizzy white hair, right? They wear thick glasses and have names like Dr. Zweistein. . . .' "

SOURCE

3-2-1 CONTACT

Magazine

THINGS TO COME

Experts Gaze into the Future

by Curtis Slepian illustrated by Nathan Jarvis

Marvin Cetron has an unusual job. He is paid to predict the future.

Cetron is a futurist—an expert who uses current information to figure out where the country and world are going, and what the future holds.

Technology is changing the world so quickly, we can't keep up. People in fields like transportation and medicine want to know about current advances *and* what advances the future may hold. That way, they can plan for tomorrow—today.

So companies are hiring futurists like Cetron to predict trends that will one day affect their products and businesses. Cetron says, "I look at technology, economics, politics and social situations and ask, 'What will the future probably look like?' "

Cetron doesn't take wild guesses. First, he gathers thousands of statistics (figures) and feeds them into big computers. Then, with the help of experts, he studies the computer read-outs and makes his forecasts.

Thinking about the future is good sense. As one futurist puts it, "In order to have the future you want, you must figure out what you want and then help create it."

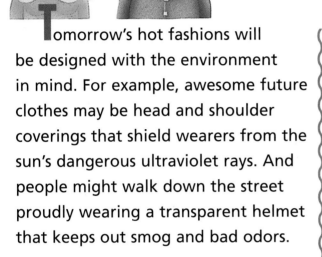

Tomorrow's hot fashions will be designed with the environment in mind. For example, awesome future clothes may be head and shoulder coverings that shield wearers from the sun's dangerous ultraviolet rays. And people might walk down the street proudly wearing a transparent helmet that keeps out smog and bad odors.

Tiny robots may perform surgery inside a patient's body. After a patient swallows the "microrobot," a human surgeon will guide it to the trouble spot. The doctor will guide it with the help of a 3-D computer simulation of the patient's insides.

Hypersonic trains will take people from New York to Los Angeles in half an hour. They might even travel across the Atlantic in an hour! How? The "trains" would travel along a tube. When air is pumped out of the tube, the trains would "fly" through the vacuum that was created.

In 30 years, it's possible that a space hotel will be open for business. Tourists will be able to take space walks and play zero-gravity sports, as well as go on side trips to the moon. Guest rooms will have artificial gravity, so taking a shower won't be a washout.

How to Market Your Invention

Do *market research* and **decide** on a name for *your* invention.

Once an inventor patents an invention, the next step is to market it. Selling a product is just one part of marketing. Naming a product, packaging it, and advertising it are also part of the marketing process. Market research plays an important part, too. Companies test products by asking potential customers for their opinions of the new product. Then they use this research to choose a name for their product.

Put on a
Jet Pak and
Take Off!

Brainstorm an Inventive Idea

Think of an invention. If you need to get your imagination working, make a wish list. For example, you might write "I wish I could fly." Now think of inventions that would make it possible for you to fly. Would sneakers with wings and a motor be a good idea? a backpack with rocket jets? a hat with a propeller? Write down several wishes and the inventive ideas that would make them come true. After you're done, look back over your list and choose the one you like the most.

Tips
- Try using alliteration or rhyme when creating a name.
- Say the names aloud to hear how they sound.

TOOLS

- notebook and pencil
- colored markers
- posterboard
- glue
- clipboard (optional)

2 Name Your Invention

Once you think of your inventive idea, it's time to give it a name. What do you want the name to say about your product? Is your invention scientific? You may want a name with a technical or scientific sounding prefix. For example, the prefixes *therma-* and *micro-* sound scientific. An invention that is meant to be fun, rather than serious, should have a name that sounds fun. Use adjectives to liven up the name of your invention. Make a list of several possible names, and then pick three of them.

SNOWEASE

Name Chart of Inventions

Boomeroom	
Jet Pak	maybe
Wing Pack	good
	good

How Am I Doing?

Take a minute to ask yourself these questions:

• Have I thought of several names for my invention?

• Have I used the information from my notes to help me choose a name?

3 Do Market Research

Take the three names you've chosen, and show them to at least six people. After they have read the names, ask them to describe what they think your invention does. Find out which name they like the best. Be sure to take notes. You may also want to look at products already being sold that are like your invention. Which product has the best name? Do you like the design of the package it comes in?

What do you like about the name and the way the product is presented? Using your market research, decide on the best name for your invention. If you want, you can also design a logo for your product.

4 Launch Your Invention

Now that you've named your invention, you're ready to launch it. Think about what kind of company would want to manufacture your invention. Ask some of your classmates to play the part of executives in a company. Then present your invention to them. Here are some things to include in your presentation.

- Make a poster with a colorful picture, the name of your invention, and some sentences describing what your product does. If you designed a logo, put that on the poster, too.

- Use the market research that you did. Tell the audience the good things that people said about your invention.

- Show a model of your invention, if you want to build one.

At the end of the presentation ask the audience for questions and suggestions.

If You Are Using a Computer ...

Create your poster with the sign or poster format. Type the name of your invention using a large fun font. You may wish to add a border and clip art to your poster. Then print it out and hang it up for everyone to see.

JET PAK

CONGRATULATIONS
You've learned that most problems have a solution. As you face new challenges, be sure to remember the problem-solving skills you've learned.

Julie Lewis
Inventor ▶

Glossary

au·to·mat·ic
(ô′tə mat′ik) *adjective*
Made to move and work without the control of a human being. He had an *automatic* bread maker.

cal·cu·la·tions
(kal′kyə lā′shənz) *noun*
The answers found by using mathematics. She checked her *calculations*.
▲ **calculation**

Word History

The word **calculation** comes from the Latin word **calculus,** which means "pebble." Small stones were used to figure out arithmetic problems.

chem·ist
(kəm′ist) *noun*
A scientist who is an expert in studying the chemical properties of substances.

en·gi·neer
(en′jə nēr′) *noun*
Someone who is trained in building structures using scientific principles.

ex·per·i·ments
(ik sper′ə mənts) *noun*
Tests to find out or prove something.
▲ **experiment**

for·mu·la
(fôr′myə lə) *noun*
An exact method for producing a particular medicine, food, or mixture.

Thesaurus

formula
recipe
method
prescription

fu·tur·ist
(fyōō′chər ist) *noun*
A person whose job is to predict future trends on the basis of current scientific knowledge.

gadg·et (gaj′it) *noun*
A small device or tool.

hy·per·son·ic
(hī′ pər son′ik) *adjective*
Traveling at least five times the speed of sound. The jet flew at *hypersonic* speeds.

im·prove·ments
(im prōōv′mənts) *noun*
Changes or additions that make something better. New windows and doors were *improvements* to the house. ▲ **improvement**

in·gen·ious
(in jēn′yəs) *adjective*
Marked by a special ability to be inventive and clever. The science project she made was *ingenious*.

in·tend·ing
(in ten′ding) *verb*
Having a purpose in mind. He was *intending* to fix his bicycle. ▲ **intend**

in·ven·tion
(in ven′shən) *noun*
Something that has been created for the first time. The telephone was Alexander Graham Bell's *invention*.

la·bor-sav·ing
(lā′bər sā′ving) *adjective*
Designed to decrease work. The washing machine is a *labor-saving* device.

li·censed
(lī′sənsd) *verb*
Granted legal permission to do something. She was *licensed* to drive a bus.
▲ **license**

log·ging (lô′ging) *verb*
Entering the necessary information to begin or end a session on a computer. ▲ **log**

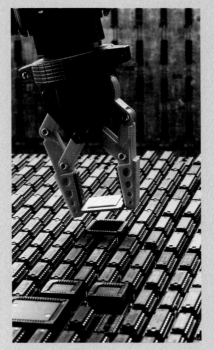
microrobot

me·chan·i·cal
(mə kan′i kəl) *adjective*
Of, or relating to, machines. They saw a *mechanical* horse at the museum.

mi·cro·chips
(mī′krō′ chips′) *noun*
Tiny electronic devices that contain circuits and components etched onto pieces of silicon.
▲ **microchip**

mi·cro·ro·bot
(mī′krō rō′ bət) *noun*
A tiny robot with specialized skills.

Word Study

The prefix **micro–** means "small." It also means "enlarging" or "amplifying." Many inventions have the prefix **micro–**. *Microphotography* reduces a picture to the size of a pinhead. The result is called a *microdot*. A *microscope* enlarges, while a *microphone* amplifies.

a	add	o͝o	took	ə =	
ā	ace	o͞o	pool	a in *above*	
â	care	u	up	e in *sicken*	
ä	palm	û	burn	i in *possible*	
e	end	yo͞o	fuse	o in *melon*	
ē	equal	oi	oil	u in *circus*	
i	it	ou	pout		
ī	ice	ng	ring		
o	odd	th	thin		
ō	open	th	this		
ô	order	zh	vision		

Glossary

mold·ed
(mōl′did) *verb*
Made or formed into a
shape. ▲ **mold**

pat·ent·ed
(pat′n tid) *verb*
Obtained a document
from the government that
gives a person the right
to be the only one who
can make and sell an
invention. The inventor
patented her invention.
▲ **patent**

Fact File

• The first United States
patent was granted in
1790.

• There are about 27
million patents on file
at the United States
Patent Office.

• Fewer than 5 percent of
all patents are ever used
or sold.

pro·gram
(prō′gram) *noun*
A sequence of coded
instructions that tell a
computer what to do.
This *program* tells the
computer how to make
graphs.

sub·stance
(sub′stəns) *noun*
The physical matter
which a thing consists of.
The *substance* in the
glass was water.

sus·pen·sion bridge
(sə spen′shun brij′)
noun
A bridge that is hung by
cables anchored to towers.

syn·thet·ic
(sin thet′ik) *adjective*
Produced by human
beings; not of natural
origin. The *synthetic*
flower looked real.

tech·nique
(tek nēk′) *noun*
A certain way of doing
things; a special method.
She had her own
technique for painting
chairs.

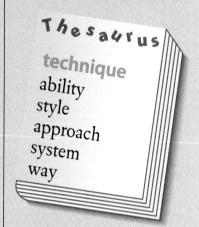

Thesaurus

technique
ability
style
approach
system
way

tel·e·phone
(tel′ə fōn′) *noun*
An instrument for talking
to people that converts
sounds into electrical
impulses that travel
through wires.

suspension bridge

ter·mi·nals
(tûr′mə nlz) *noun*
Combinations of keyboards and monitors by which information can be entered into or output by a computer.
▲ **terminal**

ther·mom·e·ter
(thər mom′i tər) *noun*
An instrument used to measure temperature.

time ma·chine
(tīm′ mə shēn′) *noun*
A fictional device that allows a person to travel back and forth in time.

tin·kered
(ting′kərd) *verb*
Made minor repairs and adjustments to something. The inventor *tinkered* with her new computer. ▲ **tinker**

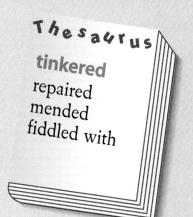

Thesaurus

tinkered
repaired
mended
fiddled with

vac·cine
(vak sēn′) *noun*
A preparation of weakened germs that is used to inoculate a person against disease. There is a *vaccine* for measles.

Word History

The word **vaccine** comes from the Latin word *vacca* which means "cow." The first vaccine ever invented was prepared from a virus that causes disease in cows. The vaccine was used to prevent smallpox.

vir·tu·al re·al·i·ty
(vûr′choo əl rē al′i tē) *noun*
Imaginary three-dimensional environments that are created by computer technology.

virtual reality

vul·can·ized
(vul′ka nīzd) *verb*
Treated rubber with a process of heat and sulfur to make it stronger and more elastic.
▲ **vulcanize**

ze·ro grav·i·ty
(zē′rō grav′i tē) *noun*
A weightless condition in which an object is not pulled by gravity.

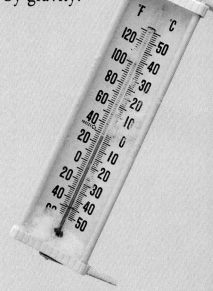

thermometer

a	add	͞o͞o	took	ə =
ā	ace	o͞o	pool	a in *above*
â	care	u	up	e in *sicken*
ä	palm	û	burn	i in *possible*
e	end	yo͞o	fuse	o in *melon*
ē	equal	oi	oil	u in *circus*
i	it	ou	pout	
ī	ice	ng	ring	
o	odd	th	thin	
ō	open	th	this	
ô	order	zh	vision	

Authors & Illustrators

Betsy Byars *pages 84–93*

Even though Betsy Byars often writes about serious issues, she manages to show the funny side of things too. Byars has said that she could never have become a writer for young people without having children of her own. "I have used thousands of things from my children's lives in my stories," she admits. However, she also says that your writing can't just be about the things you know—you've got to make up stuff!

Steven Caney *pages 32–39*

Wouldn't it be great if someone invented a contraption that makes your bed for you every morning? That someone could be you—after reading *Steve Caney's Invention Book*. Mr. Caney is a toy and game inventor who has won awards for product design. He has also written books for kids that help them design and build their own toys and games.

Judy Hindley *pages 14–31*

Judy Hindley has written over 30 books for children, many of which are nonfiction. This author grew up in California but now makes her home in England. When she is not writing, she devotes much of her free time working to end hunger in all parts of the world.

Charlotte Foltz Jones *pages 68–75*

Charlotte Foltz Jones brings her curiosity to every project she works on. She writes about things that amaze her and poses questions she'd like to have answered. In addition to *Mistakes That Worked*, this author has written a book for adults, and over one hundred magazine articles!

Robert McCloskey *pages 50–67*

Luckily for his readers, author-illustrator Robert McCloskey did not become a musician or inventor as he first thought he would. Instead, he has written and illustrated many award-winning books, often taking as many as three years to finish just one. "There are sometimes as many as 20 or 30 drawings before I turn out the one you see in the book—not completed drawings, of course, but ones finding out and exploring the best possible way of presenting a particular picture."

"No effort is too great to find out as much as possible about the things you are drawing."

Lensey Namioka *pages 100–119*

This author often uses her Chinese heritage and her husband's Japanese heritage in her writing. Her stories are almost always funny, since she feels humor is a very powerful tool. Humor helps her get her message across and entertains readers at the same time.

Books &

Author Study

More by Betsy Byars

The Cybil Wars
Two friends compete for the attention of the nicest girl in the fourth grade.

The 18th Emergency
Benjie "Mouse" Frawley has a plan for every possible emergency—or so he thinks. Then he does something to offend the biggest kid in school.

The Moon and I
In this book, Betsy Byars tells the story of her own life.

Fiction

Ahyoka and the Talking Leaves
by Peter and Connie Roop
illustrated by Yoshi Miyake
This historical novel is based on the true story of how Sequoyah and his daughter worked together to invent a syllabary for the Cherokee language.

Burton and the Giggle Machine
by Dorothy Haas
Burton decides to invent a giggle machine to cheer up his friends. He begins working on it. But who is the mysterious stranger watching him from the shadows?

Wings
by Jane Yolen
illustrated by Dennis Nolan
This retelling of an ancient Greek legend describes what happens when an inventor and his son, Icarus, attempt to fly.

Nonfiction

Be an Inventor
by Barbara Taylor
This how-to book can help get you started if you have an idea for an invention.

Great Lives: Invention and Technology
by Milton Lomask
This collection of short biographies profiles the accomplishments of many creative thinkers.

What Are You Figuring Now? A Story About Benjamin Banneker
by Jeri Ferris
This African-American inventor is famous for his discoveries in astronomy and mathematics.

Benjamin Banneker

x Media

Videos

Software

Magazines

Honey, I Shrunk the Kids
Disney

An inventor discovers that his new invention works when, by mistake, he shrinks his children. (83 minutes)

Invisible World
National Geographic Video Series. Vestron/Family Home Entertainment

Through the specialized "eyes" of high-tech cameras, this video explores unseen worlds. This presentation features microscopic cameras. (60 minutes)

Willy Wonka and the Chocolate Factory
Warner

This film, based on Roald Dahl's novel, stars Gene Wilder as the wacky inventor whose amazing machines produce wonderful candies. (98 minutes)

The Castle of Dr. Brain
Sierra OnLine
(IBM/PC, Tandy)

You're the lab assistant of Dr. Brain, who lives in a castle full of fascinating odds and ends. Work out the puzzles presented and continue on, facing increasingly difficult brain teasers along the way.

Lunar Greenhouse
MECC
(Apple II series)

Your goal is to grow food for a moon colony. To grow the largest amount, as fast as possible, you need to calculate many things—light, water, and temperature.

3•2•1 Contact
Children's Television Workshop

3•2•1 Contact examines the science in everyday life with articles about nature, sociology, and technology. It also features puzzles, fiction, and math-related activities.

Super Science Blue
Scholastic Inc.

The great activities in this magazine make it easy to apply scientific concepts to inventive ideas.

A Place to Write

Future Problem Solving Program
115 Main St., Box 98
Aberdeen, NC 28315

This program will challenge you with environmental, political, and economic problems just waiting for your solutions.

Acknowledgments

Grateful acknowledgment is made to the following sources for permission to reprint from previously published material. The publisher has made diligent efforts to trace the ownership of all copyrighted material in this volume and believes that all necessary permissions have been secured. If any errors or omissions have inadvertently been made, proper corrections will gladly be made in future editions.

Cover: Elwood Smith.

Interior: "A Piece of String Is a Wonderful Thing" from A PIECE OF STRING IS A WONDERFUL THING by Judy Hindley, illustrated by Margaret Chamberlain. Text copyright © 1993 by Judy Hindley. Illustrations copyright © 1993 by Margaret Chamberlain. Printed in the U.S. by Candlewick Press. Reprinted by permission.

"The Invention of Sneakers" and cover from STEVEN CANEY'S INVENTION BOOK. Copyright © 1985 by Steven Caney. Reprinted by permission of Workman Publishing Company, Inc. All rights reserved.

Sample letter from PUTTING IT IN WRITING by Steve Otfinoski. Copyright © 1993 by Scholastic Inc. All rights reserved. Published by Scholastic Inc. Used by permission.

"The Doughnuts" and cover from HOMER PRICE by Robert McCloskey. Copyright © 1943, renewed © 1971 by Robert McCloskey. Used by permission of Viking Penguin, a division of Penguin Books USA Inc.

Selection and cover from MISTAKES THAT WORKED by Charlotte Foltz Jones, illustrated by John O'Brien. Text copyright © 1991 by Charlotte Foltz Jones. Illustrations copyright © 1991 by John O'Brien. Used by permission of Doubleday, a division of Bantam Doubleday Dell Publishing Group, Inc.

"The Inventor Thinks Up Helicopters" and cover from THE TIGERS BROUGHT PINK LEMONADE by Patricia Hubbell, illustrations by Ju-Hong Chen. Text copyright © 1988 by Patricia Hubbell. Jacket art and illustration copyright © 1988 by Ju-Hong Chen. Reprinted with the permission of Atheneum Books for Young Readers, an imprint of Simon & Schuster Children's Publishing Division.

Diagrams from "Invent America," from January/February 1993 issue of 3-2-1 Contact America. Copyright © 1993 by Children's Television Workshop (New York, NY). All rights reserved.

"The Star Ship" and cover from THE COMPUTER NUT by Betsy Byars, cover illustration by Scott Gladden. Text copyright © 1984 by Betsy Byars. Used by permission of Puffin Books, a division of Penguin Books USA Inc. Cover illustration copyright © 1991 by Scott Gladden. Reprinted by permission of Scholastic Inc.

"The First Computers: A History Play" by Richard Chevat, from Scholastic News, January 13, 1989. Copyright © 1989 by Scholastic Inc. Reprinted by permission.

"LAFFF" and cover from WITHIN REACH, edited by Donald R. Gallo. "LAFFF" by Lensey Namioka, copyright © 1993. All rights reserved by Lensey Namioka. Cover illustration copyright © 1993 by HarperCollins Publishers. Used by permission of HarperCollins Publishers.

"Things to Come" from 3-2-1 Contact Magazine, May 1991. Copyright © 1991 by Children's Television Workshop (New York, NY). All rights reserved.

Cover from DANNY DUNN AND THE HOMEWORK MACHINE by Jay Williams and Raymond Abrashkin, illustrated by Ezra Jack Keats. Illustration copyright © 1958 by Ezra Jack Keats. Published by McGraw-Hill Inc.

Cover from EUREKA! IT'S AN AIRPLANE! by Jeanne Bendick, illustrated by Sal Murdocca. Illustration copyright © 1992 by Sal Murdocca. Published by The Millbrook Press.

Cover from ON THE BANKS OF PLUM CREEK by Laura Ingalls Wilder, illustrated by Garth Williams. Illustration copyright © 1953, renewed 1981 by Garth Williams. Published by HarperCollins Publishers.

Cover from THE REAL McCOY: THE LIFE OF AN AFRICAN-AMERICAN INVENTOR by Wendy Towle, illustrated by Wil Clay. Illustration copyright © 1993 by Wil Clay. Published by Scholastic Inc.

Photography and Illustration Credits

Photos: © John Lei for Scholastic Inc, all Tool Box items unless otherwise noted. pp. 2-3 c: © Greg Nikas/The Picture Cube. p. 2 tl, bl: © Louis Bencze for Scholastic Inc.; cl: © DEJA SHOE. p. 3 bc: © Louis Bencze for Scholastic Inc.; tc: Ana Esperanza Nance for Scholastic Inc. p. 4-6: © Ana Esperanza Nance for Scholastic Inc. p. 10 br: © Mary Evans Picture Library. pp. 10-11 tc: © Ana Esperanza Nance for Scholastic Inc.; p. 10 cl: © Dumbarton Oaks Research Library and Collections, Washington D.C.; p. 10 bl: © Science and Society Picture Library. p.11 thermometer: © Michael Holford/British Museum; cl: © The Science Museum/Science & Society Picture Library. pp. 12-13 tc: © Ana Esperanza Nance for Scholastic Inc.; p. 12 tl: © The Science Museum/Science & Society Picture Library; cr: © Michael Holford/British Museum; cl (Anna Wessels): © College of Physicians of Philadelphia; br (radio): © The Marconi Company Limited; bl (Marie Curie): © Mary Evans Picture Library. p. 13 cl (computer): © UPI/Bettman Newsphotos; bl (Walkman): © Sony Electronics; tr: © Richard Megna/Fundamental Photographs; br (games): Kermani/Gamma Liaison. p. 32 bl: © Richard Megna/ Fundamental Photographs for Scholastic Inc. p. 33 br: © courtesy Shell Chemical Company. p. 34 br, p. 35 bc: © Richard Megna/Fundamental Photographs for Scholastic Inc. p. 36 tl: © The Bettmann Archive/Goodyear Tire Co. p. 37 tr: © Richard Megna/Fundamental Graphics for Scholastic Inc.; br: © Mary Evans Picture Library. p. 38 bl: Culver Pictures; cr: © courtesy Spalding; pp. 38-39 br: © Richard Megna/Fundamental Photographs for Scholastic Inc. p. 40 c (Lewis w/plastic bottles): © Barbara Gundle/Small Planet Photography; c (Lewis w/female co-worker and w/shoes): © Louis Bencze for Scholastic Inc.; bl: © Louis Bencze for Scholastic Inc.; tc (tire): © Laine Whitcomb for Scholastic Inc.; tc (nuts & bolts): Ana Esperanza Nance for Scholastic Inc. pp. 40-41 c: © Louis Bencze for Scholastic Inc. p. 41 cr: © DEJA SHOE. p. 42 cr: © Barbara Gundle/Small Planet Photography; bl: © DEJA SHOE. p. 43 cr, bl: © Louis Bencze for Scholastic Inc. pp. 44-45: © John Lei for Scholastic Inc. p. 46 bc: © Stanley Bach for Scholastic Inc.; all others: © John Lei for Scholastic Inc. p. 47 br: © Louis Bencze for Scholastic Inc. p. 51 tl: © Richard Megna/ Fundamental Photographs for Scholastic Inc. pp. 78-79 c: © John Lei for Scholastic Inc. p. 80 br: © Stanley Bach for Scholastic Inc. p. 81 bl, tr: © Stanley Bach for Scholastic Inc.; br: © Louis Bencze for Scholastic Inc. p. 123 © John Lei for Scholastic Inc. p. 125 bl: © John Lei for Scholastic Inc. p. 126 bc: © Stanley Bach for Scholastic Inc. p. 127 bl, cr: © John Lei for Scholastic Inc.; br: © Louis Bencze for Scholastic Inc. p. 129 tc: © Steve Dunwell/The Image Bank. p. 130 bc: © John Henley/The Stock Market. p. 131 cr: © Chris Hackett/The Image Bank; bc: © Comstock, Inc. p. 132 tl: courtesy of Scholastic Trade Department; cl: courtesy of Workman Publishers; bl: © Andrew Hindley. p. 133 tr: courtesy of Charlotte Foltz Jones; br: © Don Perkins; cr: © Elaine S. Martens. p. 135 br: © Stephen Ogilvy for Scholastic Inc. p. 134 bl: © Schomburg Center for Research in Black Culture; tr: Gregory Heisler/The Image Bank.

Illustrations: pp. 8-9: Elwood Smith; pp: 10-11, 13: Tomo Narashima; pp. 48-49: Elwood Smith; pp. 68-75: John O'Brien; p. 80: Diane Blasius; pp. 82-83: Elwood Smith; pp. 84-93: Lisa Adams; pp. 94-97, 99: Dan Picasso; pp. 124-125: Diane Blasius.